The Pampered Child Syndrome
Revised Edition

of related interest

Understanding Your Two-Year-Old
Lisa Miller
ISBN 1 84310 288 9

Understanding Your Three-Year-Old
Louise Emanuel
ISBN 1 84310 243 9

Understanding 12–14-Year-Olds
Margot Waddell
ISBN 1 84310 367 2

Bringing Up a Challenging Child at Home
When Love is Not Enough
Jane Gregory
ISBN 1 85302 874 6

I'm not Naughty – I'm Autistic
Jodi's Journey
Jean Shaw
ISBN 1 84310 105 X

Divorcing Children
Children's Experience of Their Parents' Divorce
Ian Butler, Lesley Scanlan, Margaret Robinson, Gillian Douglas and Mervyn Murch
ISBN 1 84310 103 3

Achieving Best Behavior for Children with Developmental Disabilities
A Step-By-Step Workbook for Parents and Carers
Pamela Lewis
ISBN 1 84310 809 7

The Pampered Child Syndrome
Revised Edition

How to Recognize It, How to Manage It,
and How to Avoid It – A Guide
for Parents and Professionals

Maggie Mamen

Jessica Kingsley Publishers
London and Philadelphia

*This book is dedicated to AC, KC,
EH, DL, CM, and all the other
children who have had to work so hard
for the basic necessities, and for whom
a chance to be pampered would have
been a fine thing.*

Acknowledgments

Every story in this book is based on composite children from composite families, along with just a touch of poetic license. If you recognize yourself, it is because of the universality of our collective experiences, and not because I have been in your living room. Speaking with and listening to hundreds of parents and professionals (including physicians, lawyers, mediators, educators, counselors, psychologists, social workers, nurses, school secretaries) who deal with children on a daily basis, it has become increasingly obvious that the youngsters I encounter in my clinical practice are not that different from the multitudes who are out there in our schools and our communities. I am grateful to all the parents who have shared with me both the joys and the frustrations of trying to raise responsible, independent, competent, unspoiled children amid the barrage of competing values that define our current culture.

I could not have written this book without a number of important people: Gail Baird from Creative Bound, who tolerates multiple ideas that appear to be going somewhere and who is always enthusiastic on the rare occasion when they do; my colleagues at Centrepointe Professional Services, who share experiences over brown-bag lunches and keep me grounded; Sally, whose unconditional support and constructive advice are always there when needed; Audrey, whose humor and wisdom connect me with my roots; Rolf, who has taught me that there is no such word as "cannot," so that all things are possible if you are creative and willing to work hard enough, and who lets me have my space when I need it; and, of course, our three grown-up children, Natalie, Katy, and Jorin, who have become adults whom we not only love, but like, and can now pamper without anxiety.

Thank you all.

Contents

Contents

Preface

Is it truly possible for us to love our children too much? Is love really blind? Can we be so besotted with our sons and daughters that we become oblivious to the unreasonableness of their burgeoning demands on our time and energy, their relentless pressure for material goods, and their unacceptable behaviors both inside and outside the home? Do we adore and indulge them so much that our blinkers block the signs of incipient mental health disorders or behavior problems that can potentially exclude them from social acceptance, school, or perhaps even stable relationships?

We need only to look around us – in supermarkets, doctors' waiting rooms, public places, school classrooms – to recognize that this is indeed not only possible, but a fact of life, if not somewhat endemic. It is, it seems, a sign of the times, a reflection of the significant sociological pendulum swing from adult-driven parenting in the first half of the twentieth century to the current child-driven philosophies that have contributed to the construction of a teetering pedestal from which our children are now in danger of falling.

We live in a child-centered society where children's wants and demands are increasingly being given priority over marital or family harmony, financial considerations, parental sanity, common courtesy, quiet enjoyment, respect, and common sense. With the encouragement of many professionals, including some psychologists, social workers, psychiatrists, pediatricians, counselors, and others, along with the enthusiastic support of the media, manufacturers, and marketers, some children are becoming empowered to the point where parents feel helpless and ineffective. Many can no longer guarantee their children the basic building blocks of physical and mental health – sleep, nutrition, exercise, fresh air – not because they do not understand their importance, or have the ability to provide for them. Rather, they hesitate because the child does not agree, or because they are afraid of damaging a child's self-esteem. Saying "no" is interpreted by many parents as being "mean," "strict," or overly authoritarian, since they have been led to believe that imposing anything on children that children do not want to do or that makes children unhappy or uncomfortable is tantamount to abuse.

These well-intentioned parents are catering to their children's every whim and are actively avoiding, or even resisting, their responsibilities as parents to say "no," to set limits, to engender a sense of responsibility, and to teach morals, ethics, values, and the importance of family and community. Children are not learning active or creative problem-solving strategies, or how to be resilient and responsible, or how to build up a range of internal resources to manage stress, loss, failure, or disappointment. In a word, they are growing up pampered.

This book is not only about those parents who love their children deeply, who have their best interests at heart, and who work hard to provide everything they can for their families. It is also about various individuals, groups, and more global influences in our society that recommend, support, and encourage child-driven parenting practices and diagnosis-driven solutions to the problems parents are facing. Most of all, it is about children who are not simply influenced by the philosophies with which they are growing up, but who are at risk because of them.

PART I

The Pampered Child Syndrome: How to Recognize It

1

Background and Evolution

She lifts her platform shoes onto the coffee table with carefully orchestrated provocation and crosses her legs at the ankles. She studies me insolently, eyes gleaming like bright pools amidst the black mud of her eye makeup, silver tongue-stud clicking against the metal encasing her soon-to-be-perfect teeth, arms folded across her body like a small, defiant toddler. "All adults are retards," she says flatly. "Why would I want to grow up to be one? I'd rather die first."

Why indeed? She has had her first sexual encounter and her first suicide attempt. With the wisdom that these experiences have provided her, she tells me that sex isn't all it's cracked up to be; in fact, she's thinking of becoming a lesbian. She has experimented with a range of drugs, but states proudly that she doesn't do chemicals. She doesn't plan to get drunk too often because she hates not being able to remember where she was or whom she was with. She travels to raves in far-distant cities, lies barefacedly to her parents about where she is and what she's doing, and stays away for several days while her frantic mother and father die a thousand deaths. She scoffs at their concerns, and tells them that her real family, her friends on the street, will keep her safe, so why do they worry? Choosing to see neither the quiet tear brimming in her mother's eye nor the clenching of her father's cheek, she adds that, if she had indeed died from taking the Tylenol six months ago, her parents would undoubtedly be over it by now. Her grandmother passed away a couple of years ago and they hardly even mention her any more.

When I ask her if there isn't something she can think of to look forward to in the future, she wrinkles her nose and contemplates. She tells me that she can't think of anything, except perhaps learning to drive, although her Dad has already let her do that at the cottage and it's no big deal.

I have been asked to confirm the conclusion that has already been reached by significant adults in her life (her parents, her extended family, her teachers, her family physician) that she is clinically depressed and requires urgent treatment. In anticipation of this, she has already been prescribed one of the multitude of antidepressants that are becoming a rite of passage for too many young adolescents in these days of designer diagnoses. And I am expected to wave the magic wand of therapy to make everything OK.

She is 13 years old.

We might all be forgiven for speculating that she is a victim of abuse, or a neglected, abandoned youngster, deprived of essential comfort and nurturing during her formative years. Maybe she has witnessed family violence, or has an alcoholic or drug-dependent parent, or has suffered through the agonies of family breakdown. Her parents are probably miserable, or coldly authoritarian, or maybe her birth was simply a sad mistake.

The answer is "none of the above." She is the much-wanted and incredibly loved child of gentle, considerate, long-married, well-educated parents. They waited for her until they were both settled in their careers, and devoted themselves to her since the moment of conception. She was a demanding baby and they did not see how they could spread themselves more thinly to provide for additional siblings, so they chose to have no more children. Her mother stayed home with her daughter until the beginning of kindergarten, because she did not believe in delegating parenting duties to strangers. Since then, she has taken only contract work so that she can be there for field trips and bake sales, skinned knees and after-school chats. Her father has been involved in everything from piggyback rides to soccer coaching. They agreed from the beginning that they did not want to be "power parents" and risk her unhappiness, so they have deliberately chosen a parenting style that could best be described as permissive and democratic.

They tell me that she is a very gifted young lady who has been verbally adept since her first uttered syllable, and who has insisted on being part of all discussions regarding family issues. Her father has recently turned down an important and eagerly awaited promotion because she refused to move away from her friends. They have both gone out of their way to ensure that she has always been challenged and never (heaven forbid) bored. They have encouraged her to express her opinions and not to be subservient to others' demands. She has always been given a reason for whatever she has been asked to do; if the reason is one with which she does not concur, her parents have searched for another that is more persuasive. She has always been expected to make her own choices, and they have rarely countered her decisions – primarily because her wrath is something to behold. She has been provided with money for her expenses with no questions asked. They believe it is unnecessarily intrusive to monitor her spending.

Much to her parents' chagrin, she has run into a few problems in school, usually related to "attitude" and lack of respect for authority. Over the past year, she has decided to work only for teachers she likes, resulting in plummeting marks and escalating concern. She has abandoned old friendships, because, she says, her peers are much too immature, and has begun seeking out the company of older high school and university students.

Her parents have bribed her to come to this appointment, desperate for someone to help her out of her blackness. She will end up not coming back again, because she sees simply another adult whose mission in life is to prevent her from having fun. Her parents will come back because they want to know how to fix what is wrong with her. "We simply don't understand why she is so unhappy," they tell me. "We've always given her everything."

Pampered children have existed for many centuries in countries throughout the world. Notables such as Socrates, Sigmund Freud, and Alfred Adler have commented on and written about the dangers inherent in coddling children. The Chinese are currently in a quandary as to what to do about all the "Little Emperors" produced during the country's attempt to control its explosive population growth by restricting the size of families to one child only.[1] Pampered children may indeed be a single child, or they could be the youngest, or the oldest, or anywhere in between, or even every child in the family; and they may be living in a traditional two-parent situation, a reconstituted family, a single-parent home, or in a same-gender household. Most of us are fully aware of the obligation to maintain some care and control over our children's lives, particularly whilst they are still dependent and not capable of managing autonomously outside the family. Yet we often have the sense that we are given this responsibility without the authority we require in order to be effective. We wonder who has taken this away, and why we feel we need permission to parent.

As far as North America is concerned, permissive child-rearing philosophies aside for the moment, manufacturers, retailers, and advertisers have discovered that even very young children, with no purchasing power of their own, can successfully badger their parents into buying billions of dollars' worth of goods that they would otherwise not have bought. So children, especially those between the ages of 9 and 14, become a valuable marketing tool to be cultivated, empowered, and used. Children watch an average of 28 hours of television a week,[2] and in one year see approximately 10,000 commercials.[3] They then demand what commercials tell them and their parents they "need." This is the so-called "nag factor" that affects, for example, approximately 72 percent of family food purchases, let alone toys, video games, clothing, CDs, DVDs, and other specific marketing targets. In a fascinating and disturbing perspective on the predatory grooming of children as targets for advertising, Juliet Schor quotes an advertiser as saying that his company was making "…a conscious effort to move toward direct kid marketing and not even worrying about Mom. Just take her out of the equation because the nag factor is so strong…that you can just take advantage of that."[4]

Children's wish lists thus become shopping lists; and even such previously unheard of "necessities" as diapers for not-yet-willing-to-be-toilet-trained six-year-olds are suddenly considered *de rigeur*. Even more insidious is the strong message perceived by parents that to deprive a child of material goods, let alone make them do something they don't feel like doing, or something that is "boring" or not "fun," is akin to cruelty, neglect, or abuse. For those parents who are trying to set limits, marketing executives are working to undermine their authority and taking advantage of parents' innate desire for their children to be happy.[5] So the culture of indulging and pampering our children is born and sustained, despite evidence to suggest that "psychologically healthy children will be worse off if they become more enmeshed in the culture of getting and spending, and that children with emotional problems will be helped if they disengage from the worlds that corporations are constructing for them."[6]

Several thought-provoking books have already been written on the subject of indulged children and the consequences to them, their families, and society. Among them are *The Omnipotent Child* by Thomas Millar,[7] *Spoiling*

Childhood by Diane Ehrensaft,[8] and, most recently, *The Epidemic* by Robert Shaw.[9] All of these authors speak to the issue that parents need to take responsibility for setting limits that are consistent with their own value systems, as well as societal expectations, if children are going to be accepted in the world outside the family. Dr. Shaw states that parents worry so much about seeming dictatorial, squelching their children, and/or destroying their creativity, that they do not develop a repertoire of tactics to instill discipline in their children. He agrees with many of us who deal with the fallout from this *laissez-faire* philosophy that parents need to act from the very beginning as the "instruction manual" for their children, telling them how to behave, and setting up the expectation that compliance is expected. If they do not, as Dr. Shaw predicts, the children develop "an entitlement which makes it crushing to them when anyone sets limits" and learn that "the world is there as this satisfaction system that keeps doing whatever they want."[10]

So what is different about the Pampered Child Syndrome and this particular book? In the field of children's mental health, there appears to be an even more disturbing trend than simply the behavioral and societal consequences of raising a generation of overly indulged youngsters. Many of these children, before they enter my office to have the magic wand of therapy waved over them, have already been diagnosed by well-qualified, experienced medical or mental health practitioners as having a recognizable, identifiable psychiatric disorder, such as depression, anxiety, Attention Deficit Hyperactive Disorder (ADHD), bipolar disorder, and the ubiquitous Oppositional Defiant Disorder (ODD). A psychiatric diagnosis of any kind carries with it many implications, not the least of which is that the disorder must have some biological or neurological basis, and can thus potentially be treated bio-chemically. The number of prescriptions for psychotropic medication for children is increasing astoundingly, despite the fact that their central nervous systems are still developing rapidly, and the long-term effects of these medications are unknown.[11] In addition, however, a medical diagnosis strongly implies that the causes of the problem are somehow intrinsic to the individual child, whether they be biological, neurological, genetic, or by virtue of basic underlying personality or temperament. This, in turn, may lead to the assumption that there is nothing that can be done about it: "that's just how he is."

In the current climate, it is politically incorrect to suggest that we parents may have something to do with how our children behave, because this is "blaming" us, and this makes us feel even more guilty than we do already. There is little question that raising children is a two-way street. We do certain things; a child responds a certain way. If we like the way the child responds, we may do the same thing the same way again. We may or may not get the same response from the child a second time. Given that our children are all different from each other, even identical twins, and given that they respond in a broad range of different ways to exactly the same situations, it is simplistic, naive, and even just plain wrong, to assume that there is one, and only one, right way to parent. There is, therefore, no definitive list of strategies that will always work, nor any possibility of creating a recipe for the "correct" way to raise a child. Nor is there a way that is "wrong;" obviously as long as we are behaving in a reasonably humanistic way, and not being cruel, abusive, or neglectful, regardless of headlines that scream such statements as: "A child expert tells us why we are doing it all wrong."[12] There is little that will erode parental confidence as effectively as the belief that there must be a proper way to do it and we simply don't know it yet. The fact is that some strategies will work for some children some of the time. There is simply nothing that will work for all children all of the time. And no "expert" will ever know our children better than we do.

The one thing that is clear is that, as loved and trusted authority figures, parents have an *obligation* to make the decisions that will guide our children, socialize them, and eventually teach them to be independently functioning adults. If we don't, no one else will. If we don't know how to do this, we need to find out, and in the meantime we have to pretend we do. We need to be aware of the values we want to teach and the choices that we make when we parent, and we need to be prepared to live with the consequences of those choices. Then we can accept responsibility, not blame. If we have made choices that have not resulted in the consequences we expected, we are wasting our time if we continue to look back and beat ourselves up. As with everything else, we can learn from this, and make different choices in the future. It is pretty clear to most of us that our children are bombarded with multiple influences, not simply ours alone, and that our job of shaping their values becomes more difficult as society becomes increasingly complex.

As parents, one of the choices we are quite likely to make from time to time will be to indulge our offspring. We feel mellow. We feel generous. We enjoy the warm, fuzzy feelings we get from providing the little extras that our children enjoy. And we love our children, so we strive not only to do whatever we can to satisfy their every want and need, but also to surprise them with treats that they have neither demanded nor expected. Besides which, it is so easy to parent when our children are happy and content with us and with what we are asking them to do. We ourselves are not very different from the rats in the maze who will take the same direction over and over, provided there is a reward at the finish line. If it feels good, we'll do it. Just like our children. We also know what it feels like to be pampered once in a while, whether this is an unexpected gift, a loving gesture, a special treat, or a full-blown excursion to the spa of life with all of our needs being met by someone who cares deeply for us. We certainly need to give ourselves permission to indulge both our children and ourselves from time to time. So what's the problem?

A former colleague of mine told the story of discovering three cute, adorable raccoon babies at the cottage, and feeding them bread on her porch. They turned up religiously each evening at sundown; she enjoyed watching them and playing with them, and they enjoyed the food. One day, she discovered that she had no bread to give them. Much as she tried to explain to the raccoons the reason why she couldn't ante up, they simply refused to take "no" for an answer. She tried to find alternative reasons they would accept; she tried offering them raccoon food; she apologized; she groveled; she even tried being firm. They simply bared their teeth and advanced on her aggressively until she had no option but to turn, run, and lock herself inside for several hours while they noisily attempted to claim what they clearly perceived as their entitlement. She subsequently avoided going to the cottage for a number of weeks afterwards until they had apparently given up, wandered away, and found a new source to pamper them. Or perhaps they died trying.

Apart from the obvious environmental caveat about feeding animals in the wild, the main moral of this story is clear. Once we become accustomed to being pampered, it loses its "special" feeling, and becomes an expectation which we will then insist on being met. Meantime, and more importantly, we may not have developed any means of surviving without it, and we will then not be prepared to exist in the jungle of the real world outside the family.

The Pampered Child Syndrome is a term that includes both parent and child factors that have their roots in well-intentioned child-rearing philosophies, yet that seem to come together to create "symptoms" that frequently meet the checklist criteria for many well-known psychiatric and psychological diagnoses. Even in the absence of the more serious diagnoses, most of us recognize behaviors and attitudes that alert us to the possibility that our children are acting somewhat over-indulged or spoiled, and want to do something to prevent the situation getting out of hand.

If we are teachers, we are frequently in the unique position of being the first authority figures that children encounter outside the family. We can readily identify children who have been pampered at home, who simply do not recognize either societal hierarchies, or the fact that they need to be accountable for their own choices and behaviors, and who expect prompt and efficient service. Although we may sometimes feel we are swimming upstream against the tide of child-centered parenting philosophies, we have a better chance than almost anyone else of providing the kind of experiential environment for children that can prepare them for life in the real world.

The role of professionals is a critical component in the development of the Pampered Child Syndrome. If we fail to recognize the behaviors of overly pampered children, and to identify the contributing factors, this may sometimes lead to over-diagnosis of psychiatric disorders and the prescription of inappropriate and potentially dangerous treatments, including unnecessary medication. In addition, there may well be long-term, far-reaching consequences, not only for the individual and his or her family, but also for the drain that these children cause on the health and education systems in times of financial constraint where precious funding needs to be conserved for truly legitimate cases.

This book does not claim, or even attempt, to provide all the answers; rather, it encourages us to ask questions and to look at our own contributions. It examines some of the choices we have, the values we try to teach, the messages we send, and the ways they are sometimes received. Although the outlook may sometimes seem discouraging, the fact is that when we change what we do and stick with it, we can often effect change in others, even in others who appear to be quite resistant to changing. As the most significant adults in our children's lives, we need not only to acknowledge, but also accept responsibility for, the consequences of our choices as parents, so that we can make our own decisions as to whether we are prepared to live with them, along with the behavior our children will potentially exhibit. If we do not like what we see, we can learn to feel confident to do something differently to bring back a healthy balance in the family, and to provide our children with both the nurturing *and* the guidance they need.

Notes

1. Jones, G. (2000) "China's Little Emperors." *The Independent on Sunday: The Sunday Review.* 12 November. London: Independent Newspapers.
2. Issue Brief Series (1997) *How Children Process Television.* Studio City, CA: Mediascope Press.

3. Issue Brief Series (2000) *Children, Health and Advertising.* Studio City, CA: Mediascope Press.

4. Schor, J.B. (2004) *Born to Buy: The Commercialized Child and the New Consumer Culture.* New York: Scribner, pp.24–25.

5. Linn, S. (2004) *Consuming Kids: The Hostile Takeover of Childhood.* New York: The New Press.

6. Schor, J.B. (2004) *Born to Buy: The Commercialized Child and the New Consumer Culture.* New York: Scribner, p.167.

7. Millar, T.P. (1983) *The Omnipotent Child: How to Mould, Strengthen and Perfect the Developing Child.* Vancouver, BC: Palmer Press.

8. Ehrensaft, D. (1997) *Spoiling Childhood: How Well-Meaning Parents Are Giving Children Too Much – But Not What They Need.* New York: The Guilford Press.

9. Shaw, R. (2004) *The Epidemic: The Rot of American Culture, Absentee and Permissive Parenting, and the Resultant Plague of Joyless, Selfish Children.* New York: Regan Books.

10. Ward, B. (2004) "Dealing with Brats." Interview with Dr. Robert Shaw for "The Citizen's Weekly." *Ottawa Citizen.* 8 February.

11. Kluger, J. (2004) "Medicating Young Minds." *Time Magazine (Canadian edition).* 19 January.

12. Ward, B. (2004) "Dealing with Brats." Interview with Dr. Robert Shaw for "The Citizen's Weekly." *Ottawa Citizen.* 8 February.

2

Pampered Children

We have known for a long time that there are certain factors essential to children's physical and mental health and well-being: sufficient sleep, good nutrition, fresh air, exercise, nurturing, safety, and security. There is, somehow, something uncomfortable, maybe even unethical, about trying to find ways to deal with behavioral, emotional, or even learning difficulties through therapy or medical treatments if these basic building blocks are not firmly in place. How can a child, or any one of us, come to that, cope with even the normal stresses of everyday life if the mind/body machine is not well-lubricated, tuned up, and fully ready to function? Yet, parents are often heard to say: "He simply refuses to eat breakfast," "We can't get her to go to bed at a reasonable hour," "He has become such a couch potato!" or "She just won't wear a bike helmet." These statements are worrying enough if the children are in their teens. But what if they are three or four years old? What if they have no energy to learn? Or are falling asleep in class? Or are becoming obese? Or if they sustain a head injury that takes away their future? "But how can we *make* him?" say the parents. "We've tried everything, and nothing works." It always seems a little odd when parents wonder why they cannot get a child to do homework or the dishes, when they cannot make him do something upon which his safety, or even his life, actually depends.

It is tempting to think that parents such as these perhaps do not care for their children that much, or that they are neglectful or inconsiderate or dismissive. However, closer scrutiny usually indicates that this is far from the truth. In fact, most of these parents place their children's well-being and happiness way above their own, and would do pretty much everything to ensure that their children are comfortable, safe, and protected. They have a set of philosophies and values about child-rearing that most of us have for our own families. We all want to raise children who:

- are comfortable and happy
- are stimulated and enriched
- can make their own choices
- are included in family decisions
- are given reasons for the things they are asked to do
- are treated equally and fairly
- can express their feelings and be heard
- have positive self-esteem.

These aspirations are hard to argue with. It is difficult to imagine telling someone not to worry about any of these. And, although we might quibble about degree, there is not one of them that we would consider inappropriate or likely to do a child harm.

These goals become the messages that we send to our children. The messages are sent consistently, consciously, and directly; they are modeled and reinforced; they become entrenched in family practices; and are part of the fabric of daily life.

However, it is always important to recognize that, in order to understand the degree of communication of information, it is necessary to ascertain whether the message *received* is the same as the message that was *sent*. In many instances, there is a tendency for children to perceive things a little differently than we intended; so when we check it out, we often find slight misinterpretations of what we originally had in mind to communicate. This is where the problems begin (see the table on the next page).

Without any effort, we have managed to set our children off on the road paved with good intentions, and we all know where that leads. The ease with which our messages become distorted and the speed with which they become hard-wired can be record-breaking. So before we know it, we have planted the seeds of the Pampered Child Syndrome. And then we water and fertilize them.

What we say ...	What children hear...
We want our children to be happy and comfortable.	I should always be happy and comfortable. When I experience loss or failure, or feel sad, upset, frustrated, or disappointed, someone should make me feel better.
We want our children to be stimulated and enriched.	I should never be bored. I should only be asked to do things that are stimulating and enriching, not things that are tedious and boring. In fact, if it's not interesting, I won't do it.
We want our children to make their own choices.	No one should tell me what to do; I should be allowed to make up my own mind.
We want our children to be included in family decisions.	Adults should not make any decisions without consulting me first. I should be part of the management team.
We want our children to be given reasons for things that they are asked to do.	I will not do anything unless you give me a reason why I should. It must be a good reason. If I don't agree with the reason, you have to keep looking to find one that I do agree with.
We want our children to be treated equally and fairly.	I should be treated the same as adults. If other people can do it, I should be able to do it too.
We want our children to express their feelings and be heard.	I should never do anything unless I feel like doing it. Are you listening? Did you not hear what I said?
We want our children to have positive self-esteem.	I should always feel good about myself.

How we pamper

The good servant

When Alfred Adler talked about "pampering," he was referring to parents, primarily mothers, who did everything for their children. By doing so, he claimed, children were deprived of the opportunity to develop coping skills and problem-solving strategies of their own, instead remaining dependent on parents or other adults, and demanding of the attention they required in order to function on a daily basis. This may have been many decades ago, but we have not come very far.

Kristina, 12, is treasured by her mom, who sees her as a very special legacy from a brief, casual, long-ago affair with a married boss. Her mom has dedicated herself to proving to her own parents that she can manage to be a good mother, despite their doubts that she is mature enough to handle the responsibilities. She tries to make sure Kristina is always clean, tidy, and well-dressed, even though her minimum-wage job leaves little money available for anything other than the basic necessities of life which, according to her daughter, include designer jeans. She does all the laundry, grocery shopping, cleaning, cooking, along with all other household-related tasks, and in her spare time is chauffeur and handyperson. Whenever she asks her daughter to help, she is greeted at best with a withering look and at worst with a torrent of verbal abuse; so she does not ask. She says that, although she doesn't really like the tantrums, at least she doesn't get bitten or hit very often any more, the way she did when Kristina was younger. Even when she is sick in bed with one of her migraines, she makes sure she is up early enough to get Kristina off to school with her lunch all made and her bag all packed. She sits with her every evening through the homework ritual, often typing notes, book reports, and projects on the computer because they have to be done and Kristina gets upset if she's asked to do them herself. She has given up trying to get her to bed on time, and just lets her watch TV or chat on the phone or computer until her own bedtime. This is not very convenient, because she really needs to use the phone or computer herself, but she does not ask. Kristina has told her she should get her own, but it will be a while because money is a little tight at the moment.

Kristina is beginning to have trouble at school. She rarely finishes her classroom work, although her homework is always completed and handed in on time. She has problems keeping track of her notes and binders, comes to class without the books she needs, has not done well on class tests, and never shows much interest in anything she does. Her teachers say she has "attitude," and that she is beginning to have some social problems with her classmates. They are planning to call her mother in for a meeting so that they can explain to her that she needs to be more involved at home, making sure Kristina is better organized. They are sure this will solve the problem.

The bottomless pit

Like your children, I'm sure, there was a time when our son believed that the way we got our money was to go to the bank machine, put in a plastic card, and out came $20 bills. We could hardly blame him; this is indeed what we did. If there was no money in the house, we simply went to the machine to get more. Even when we explained to him about the proverbial money tree, he would look at us with the same benignly skeptical look he reserved for stories about the Easter Bunny and the Tooth Fairy. It wasn't really until he got his first paying job and the allowance dried up that he began to understand that the machine needed to be topped up once in a while. Children also take a while to recognize that everything has a price. The TV commercials never talk about how much things cost; only that you don't have to pay for the next 12 months to refurnish your house. You can get zero percent financing for the newest luxury vehicles, and we all know that zero equals nothing. We are bombarded with messages that, if we really love our children, we will buy them this, get them that, and never make them feel rejected by their social circle because they do not have the latest video game or whatever toy everyone else has. For those who are separated or divorced, there is the added concern that if we don't cough up, the other parent will. So we shower our children with material goods because this is what good parents do, often resulting in what has been termed "affluenza," which is now approaching epidemic proportions.

Jackie talks about Jamie's fourth birthday. She says that she had bought him so many presents that he didn't even finish opening half of them before he got bored. She had been a little embarrassed when he cried after he opened his grandma's gift and had seen it was just clothes. Her mother-in-law had been pretty upset, and had hinted that he was an ungrateful, spoiled brat. But surely she should know that clothes are no present for a four-year-old. She's not short of cash; she could have bought him something a bit more appropriate. Jackie herself had been shopping for months, picking up this and that when she saw something she knew Jamie would just love. She is proud of the fact that she has a good eye for a bargain, and rarely buys something that is not on sale. Her husband has asked why she has bought another remote-controlled truck when Jamie already has four or five or six, she can't remember. He simply doesn't appreciate that children get tired of new toys really quickly, so you have to keep getting them something that they'll enjoy. Besides which, it was half price. The only problem is that they're running out of storage space for the children's things, because, even though Jessica is only two, she's already got so much stuff that they have nowhere to put it all. Jackie is beginning to worry, because they start showing the Christmas commercials right around Halloween, and Jamie has already begun to tell them what he wants. She has tried persuading him to give away some of his toys to children who don't have very much, but he just doesn't want to and, well, they are his, after all, aren't they? So, they're going to renovate the basement to provide some more storage space. And make sure that her mother-in-law has a copy of Jamie's wish list next time.

The lion, the lioness, and their cubs

Doing everything for a child and going overboard with material goods are two very familiar ways of pampering children. We've pretty much all been there and done that. However, there are other, less obvious ways by which we give children the message that we want life to be comfortable for them, regardless of the cost. One of the main ones is that we make excuses for their behavior, and by doing so prevent them from experiencing the consequences of the very choices we are trying to encourage them to become competent at making. For whatever reasons, we simply cannot let our children be uncomfortable, and facing up to something they have done wrong is highly likely to cause discomfort. They may also feel bad, upset, guilty, embarrassed, humiliated, for whatever they have done, and they may even have to pay a penalty that involves some deprivation, restitution, inconvenience, even pain of some kind. They may have known about this consequence before they did whatever they did, and made the conscious choice to do it anyway. Or they may genuinely not have realized that their actions would result in someone's displeasure or wrath. In our efforts to prevent their discomfort, we intervene with every good intention. We want to teach them to consider the consequences of their behavior; but we end up teaching them something else entirely.

Peter had been picked up by the police, caught red-handed with a can of spray paint beside some still-dripping graffiti underneath the underpass near his home. His friends had seen the police cruiser approaching and had tried to warn him as they were running off, but his headphones were blasting music and he hadn't heard them. The cop wasn't into listening to him explain that it wasn't his paint, or that some guy he didn't know had shoved it in his hand as he ran away, or that the beer he had in his pocket he was actually carrying for his older brother. It wasn't the nice cop who had just told him to take off the last time he'd been in the wrong place at the wrong time. It was the creep who had been harassing him and his friends every single time he saw them on the street. This was such a small town, you couldn't even have a good time with your buddies without some cop in your face. At least he'd been taken home, not to the police station. His dad hadn't been too pleased at being woken up at midnight. He listened to the cop's version of what had happened, then told him that Peter's mom had run off five years ago, and that the boys had not been the same since. He'd been working two jobs to try to make ends meet, and the boys' friends were wandering the streets at all hours, and were a bad influence. The school didn't help; the teachers simply didn't care any more, and the idiot principal had suggested that Peter not go back next semester. Talk about dodging responsibility. He paid his taxes and he knew he had the right to have his kids in school. He promised the police officer that he'd make sure his son didn't do anything like that again, and the cop left – finally! Peter trusted his dad. Dad understood that you couldn't rat out your friends; he'd always taught the boys that loyalty was important. He knew that there were precious few places for the kids to go to have fun, and he thought it was ridiculous that they would bother about a 17-year-old with one beer in his jacket. Plus, he recognized Peter's artistic talents and said that it wasn't as if the graffiti had been crude or in bad taste. As for the beer, surely they knew that all the guys liked a drink once in a while. It's sad, he told his son, that the police had nothing better to do than to disturb law-abiding people when they should be out catching real criminals. Why didn't they just split the beer and then get to bed?

"Whatever!"

A tried-and-true strategy for any one of us to use to get our own way involves sheer determination and persistence. From basic psychological principles, we know that the most powerful and effective method to ensure that a behavior will continue to occur is to reinforce it sporadically. This is why I offer my husband a second piece of pie about a dozen times, even though he has politely refused the initial suggestion. After "Would you like a piece of pie?" and the first "No, thanks" follow increasingly persuasive reasons why he should give in. "But it's your favorite!" "But there are only a couple of pieces left." "But I baked it especially for you." "But I spent all morning in the kitchen." "But it'll go bad." "But there are children starving in Ethiopia." "Well, I'll just have to throw it out." Sooner or later, worn down by his inability to find acceptable reasons for sticking with his original decision, he says: "Oh, OK." And I know that, the next time, I shall have to ask him at least a dozen times before he gives in. Our own children become experts at this game very early on in life as they cash in on our tiredness, our guilt, our low tolerance for their unhappiness, and our need to be liked.

Jean-Claude and Suzanne are seeking help because their marriage is on the verge of disintegrating. Their two young children are "out of control," mealtimes are a nightmare, and they are all getting little or no sleep. Babysitters refuse to return. Relatives are increasingly unavailable to watch the children. Jean-Claude complains that they have no time together as adults and haven't been sleeping in the same bed for months, so their love life is all but dead. Suzanne counters with the accusation that, if he were home more often and would help her with the children, she would not always be so tired and then maybe she'd feel more like being a wife again. They have tried to establish a regular bedtime routine for their five- and three-year-olds, but it has stretched into a three-hour harangue that leaves everyone exhausted.

They decided very early on in their parenting that they did not believe in "power parenting." They have read all the books they can find, discarding any that espouse what they see as an authoritarian approach, and hanging on to every word of those that value talking so children will listen and taking a child-centered approach where children are not made to do anything for which they are not completely ready. And willing. So far, they have not been able to find a good enough reason that the children will accept to get them either to go to bed when they should, or to eat whatever they are served for meals. They tell them why they should, and the children simply don't agree. They find another approach, but that doesn't work either. Pretty soon, they run out of options. So they give in. The result is that the children wander the house until they fall asleep, usually in their parents' bed, and refuse to eat anything that is put in front of them, whining and screeching until they are given what they want so that they will quiet down. Suzanne and Jean-Claude each try to placate and to reason with the children, but usually run out of steam or patience or both, either with the children or with each other.

Jean-Claude has begun to spend more and more time at work, taking shifts that keep him away from the house in the evenings and even on the weekends. Suzanne would love to return to work, but Jean-Claude will not agree to take parental leave, and she cannot find anyone else who will look after the children. Besides which, she feels very guilty when she thinks of leaving them with someone else. Children need their own parents to raise them, not some strangers who really don't care. Daycare centers are regimented. Home daycare providers, even the good ones, have to cater to other children as well and may not have enough time or attention to go around. They tried having someone come to the house to help out, but got tired of people who found some excuse not to come back, or who didn't seem to understand that you couldn't make children do things they didn't want to do, or who were simply much too strict. Suzanne is now worried about finding an appropriate school for their older child because they all seem to be very set in their ways about how to deliver education, and don't cater to children's individual needs or learning styles.

Unfortunately, in our efforts to pamper our children, we often forget that our primary job is to prepare them for the real world outside the family, keeping them safe and healthy, and ensuring that they learn appropriate social behaviors that will serve to foster independence as they journey into adulthood. We know that raising children in an environment where they become dependent on adult attention and indulgences neither reflects reality outside the family nor fosters independence, and thus does not provide them with the resilience or the tools necessary for survival. Yet we want to nurture and care for them; we need to, and they need us to. Why, then, do we go overboard to pamper them and unwittingly inhibit their healthy development?

Why we pamper

We must look toward many sources in order to begin to understand how we have come to the point of believing that we will somehow be harming our children if we say no once in a while. My own parents and their generation were products of the late Victorian era, before the advent of child psychology, when the notion of "adolescence" had not yet been coined, and when children were definitely to be seen and not heard. We post-war children were wanted and loved, and our needs were met as best they could be, given the belief systems of the times. We were born to parents who were grateful to have survived the Depression, wars, holocausts, genocide, and the advent of nuclear weapons. Children were valued highly, but the philosophies of the behaviorist movement, where the child was believed to be a *tabula rasa*, a blank slate that could be molded and formed by parents, were the order of the day. We were fed on a four-hour schedule, regardless of whether or not we were hungry, and we had regular nap times and bedtimes, regardless of whether or not we were tired. Food was rationed in many countries, and we therefore had little or no choice about what was served for meals. In school, we were never consulted about our feelings about how we learned, and the notion of individual learning styles would have been laughable to our teachers, who were facing classes of 40 or more as the first huge wave of Baby Boomers moved through the system.

In the 1950s, with the advent and rapid spread of television, the popular press, and other mass media, the views and values of a range of child-centered child-rearing specialists became available for the first time. Dr. Spock and his permissive approach to children's behavior ruled. With the "all you need is love" mantra of the 1960s, the idea grew that freedom of expression was sacred, and the "pigs" of authority were to be vanquished. We were all flower children together in the early 1970s, and the boundary between childhood and adulthood was bridged by adolescence and became blurred. Then came Watergate, with the message that even the highest powers were vulnerable and could be brought down, just as David slew Goliath. From that moment, we all learned that authority could never again simply be trusted, but should always be questioned. Our own parliamentary system permitted live television cameras into the House of Commons to witness and broadcast our elected elite heckling, swearing, interrupting, hurling insults, arguing for the sake of arguing, and generally being rude to each other, breaking the most basic rules of respectful behavior.

As a fallout from the Civil Rights movements of the 1960s, 1970s, and 1980s, the General Assembly of the United Nations adopted in 1989 the Convention on the Rights of the Child,[1] which was later translated by UNICEF into a child-friendly version.[2] This bill of rights was obviously intended to protect the children of the world from exploitation, cruelty, inhumane conditions, and abuse, and includes such basic rights as the right to life, food, clothing, a safe place to live, education, protection, and to have basic needs met. Some rights are more ambiguous, and seem to apply more to a middle-class society for whom the fundamentals of existence are not only a given, but are very much taken for granted. These include the right to privacy, the right to have adults listen to and take your opinions seriously, the right to choose your own friends, and the right to get information from radio, newspaper, books, computers, and other sources. While these "rights" are tempered with such statements as the need for adults to "make sure that the information you are getting is not harmful," it is not difficult to see how parents may be persuaded that we are depriving our children of their rights by setting limits on freedom of expression, freedom of association, and access to information. Following the UN's initiative, there were many other attempts at bills of rights for children, many composed by the empowered children themselves. One of these, called The Children's Bill of Rights,[3] somewhat amusingly included the right to "listen to music of their choice," "to have pocket money," and essentially to be treated exactly the same as adults. It was interesting and thought-provoking recently to be involved in discussion with a group of elementary and high school principals concerning pampered children, and hearing them agree how much their students had changed over the past 15 years. Who knows whether it is merely coincidence that it was exactly 15 years ago that the United Nations spearheaded the issue of children's rights. And who argues with the United Nations?

As the last century drew to a close, we had been exposed to the horrific legacy of child abuse that seemed to be rampant everywhere, including our national institutions such as schools and churches. We were more aware than ever of not wanting to be seen as mean, punitive, authoritarian, neglectful, controlling, or abusive. With the dawn of the millennium, many of us have more money and a better lifestyle than our parents; we are bombarded with messages urging us to be thinner, fitter, faster, better, smarter, richer; and we want to pass on our good fortune to our children.

It is human nature for parents to move heaven and earth to avoid children's discomfort and pain. This is what we are here for. It is our job to keep them safe and healthy, and to kiss it better. We find it very difficult to tolerate our children being angry with us. Who has not reeled under the fire of "I hate you!" "You are the meanest mother in the world!" "Nobody else's parents ever make them do that!" "I wish I didn't live in this family!" "You're not my real dad!"? When we are already uncertain about whether our parenting is at least adequate, the last thing we need is for the recipients of our ministries to verbalize to the world our worst fears about our performance. If we ourselves have grown up in a family that was authoritarian, punitive, alcoholic, or abusive, we are most likely to do whatever we can to avoid someone being angry at us, even if that someone is a red-faced, irate two-year-old. We flash back to when we were four, or ten, or fifteen. How can we parent effectively at that point, when we are children ourselves? Sometimes, we are afraid of our own angry response, thinking that we may be unable to control ourselves and risk harming someone, by physical assault or verbal barrage. The result is that many of us will do whatever we can to avoid our children's anger. We will back off, reduce our expectations, change the rules, give them what they want. A child who is pleased with us is a child who is easy to parent.

Another common reason for giving in to children's demands is to save time. It is frequently far easier to go along with what a child wants, rather than to take the time to go through the stresses and strains of arguing. It is also much quicker and easier to do something for a child, rather than to wait for a child to do a less-than-perfect, often somewhat slow job. This applies to everything from helping a toddler get dressed ("Me do it!") to doing the vacuuming for a reluctant teen. Children catch on to this very quickly, and naturally take the easy route. Pretty soon, it becomes a pattern. Waiting parents out becomes the children's pastime. How long can Dad stand it before he tidies the living room himself? When will Mom give in and shovel the driveway?

Today's busy parents are extraordinarily guilt-ridden when it comes to spending quality time with children. We set out for work early, work long hours, leave our children in the care of others, rush home late, and then spend the rest of the evening trying to make up for depriving our children of our valuable company. They don't ask to go to bed, so we keep them up late, often until they are tired beyond reason. We hover over homework so that we can feel "involved" in their school work. We let them watch TV or play on the computer, because they are then happy with us, and we don't have to feel so badly about being the Me-Generation that takes good care of Number One. The more we give them, the more our children's demands for goods and services increase. They can sense our guilt the way our labrador senses food. Parents who stay at home full-time with the children fare no less well. Their children are supremely attuned to guilt. "Why would you make me do my own laundry when you're home all day doing nothing?" is the way one particularly adroit 13-year-old articulates this issue. The basic message our children give us is: "You gave birth to me. I didn't ask to be born. You owe me." So pay up we do.

One of the most powerful reasons why we pamper our children, whether it be by ministering to their every need, buying them material goods, protecting them, or giving in, is to attempt to compensate for something we have experienced in our own lives. Most frequently, this has to do with our own parents, and how we perceive we were raised. We conveniently forget that we were born in different times, with different value systems and different views of child-rearing. If our parents did not appear to care how we felt, this was usually a reflection of their socio-cultural context, and not of their levels of compassion as human beings. Whether this is or is not the case, however, we may genuinely struggle to avoid being overly punitive, or verbally abusive, or explosive. We may make statements like: "I swore I would never raise my voice to my children the way my dad did," or "My mother would ignore me for days; I'm never going to ignore my children."

Children of divorce or separation are often the subject of compensatory pampering. We've all read the books and the studies; we are all trying our best to avoid harming our children because our marital relationship has failed. Many parents these days seek therapeutic or counseling help in order to try to prevent their children feeling the sting of the separation. There is frequently a conscious effort on the part of parents to over-compensate so that the children do not feel the pain of loss. Sometimes, however, the pampering is a result of an effort to outdo the other parent – to win the "contest" as to who can provide the better environment for the child.

Lisa is the only child of two professional parents who have been divorced for as long as she can remember. Like so many children, she spends equal time with both her father and her mother, traveling back and forth every Sunday evening. Her parents want to make sure that they devote themselves to her whenever she's in their home, so each of them puts the rest of life on hold every second week. Relationships, hobbies, friends, meetings, doctors' appointments, work assignments – everything is rescheduled to the week when she's not with them. The result is that Lisa has had 100 percent parental attention at all times.

When she was little, she got very used to this, and became distraught if anyone or anything interrupted her time with them. Both parents still dread the day when they might have to break it to her that there is a budding relationship in the offing. In fact, her mom actively avoids such involvement, because she knows that Lisa will not tolerate it. Her father religiously hides his long-time girlfriend, making her remove all traces of her presence every alternate week. Now Lisa is 15. The last thing she wants is to have 100 percent parental attention, and fights what she sees as their over-involvement in her life, although she doesn't really know how to survive without it; so she is angry and confused most of the time. She looks at her parents and sees two adults who apparently have no friends, no relationships, no hobbies, no life. She's not sure she wants to grow up to be like them. At the stage of development where she needs to start to discover her own self, she is tired of moving back and forth between two homes, and yearns to settle in one place. Her mom and dad have told her that she is free to make the choice, and are currently engaged in a bidding war to see who wins Lisa's company full-time. As we go to press, mom has offered to allow her to have her boyfriend stay over on weekends, which her dad says will be over his dead body, and dad has held out the carrot of driving lessons and a new car when she gets her license. Mom has thrown in a holiday in the Caribbean for Lisa and her best friend, but wait! Dad is considering providing a season's ski pass and a $50 per week allowance, no strings attached. Mom is furious at this blatant example of trying to "buy" their daughter, and indicates that she will pull a few strings to find Lisa a part-time job so that she can earn money with dignity. Lisa has mentioned that she is leaning toward living with Mom, and Dad is asking for some urgent therapy for her so that she can make the right choice and live with him. Stay tuned.

Finally, one of the most compelling reasons why we give in to our children and indulge them is to be liked. When it comes down to it, there are few of us who would volunteer to be disliked. When children like us, they will be more compliant. When we are liked, we will be more generous. This situation can easily be mutually satisfactory. The main problem is that children will certainly *not* like us when we ask them to do things they do not want to do, or things they find tedious or boring, or things that are difficult or stressful. Nor when we cause short-term pain, even though we can foresee the longer-term gain. Nor when we ask them to wait for something they want right away. Nor when we say no.

Do we all give in to our children from time to time? Of course we do. Do we all do things to keep the peace? Yes, indeed. We usually provide a healthy balance to these lapses and indulgences, and somehow manage to tread the middle ground. When we back down, make excuses, give in, roll over, and play dead, time after time after time, however, the longer-term effects can be devastating. The bread is gone, and the baby raccoons approach with their teeth bared.

Notes

1. United Nations Convention on the Rights of the Child (1989) www.unicef.org/ crc/crc.htm
2. Department of Canadian Heritage, Human Rights Program (1991) *Convention on the Rights of the Child.* Ministry of Supply and Services Canada. Obtainable from Rights-Droits@pch.gc.ca
3. Children's Bill of Rights (CBOR) Secretariat (1996) *The Children's Bill of Rights.* Obtainable from www.kidlink.org/KIDFORUM/

3

The Pampered Child Syndrome

Angela's parents love her totally and unconditionally. She's sweet, sensitive, and a free spirit, with a wonderfully creative imagination. She cries whenever she feels "pressured," so they don't pressure her. They just want her to be happy, and so they let her do pretty much whatever she wants to do at home. She says she's bored in school, so they have asked her teacher to provide her with some enrichment activities.

Angela is six, does not pay attention in class, cannot sit still for circle time, is having difficulty acquiring basic reading, printing, and math skills, and simply does not do her assigned work at school. Her pediatrician has prescribed medication to address what he and Angela's teacher believe is an "Attention Deficit Hyperactive Disorder."

Jeff is the youngest son of affluent parents. He has always been a bit demanding and would never take "no" for an answer, says his mother, but "he's the baby after all, and so cute that you just can't help giving in." He has had many temporary hobbies and interests, which his parents have supported enthusiastically, but lately he has withdrawn from all of his former activities and is hanging around with friends his parents have never met. They feel very guilty about the long hours they spend at work, and want to ensure that they make up for any unhappiness they have caused their children. Jeff is struggling in his last year of high school, and can't decide what he wants to do next.

Jeff is 17 and has everything, including an affinity for smoking pot and drinking alcohol. He has recently been diagnosed by his family physician as "clinically depressed," and placed on an antidepressant, as well as a sleeping medication.

> Paul's parents have always expected him to make his own decisions, to be self-sufficient, to question everything, and to take initiative whenever possible. They deliberately stay away from telling him what is right or wrong because they know he is intelligent, and they want him to make up his own mind. They intervene when other adults try to impose their views on him, and defend him rigorously whenever he is criticized. They admire and encourage his ability to stand up for himself.

Paul is 13, bright, and a bully. He has no respect for authority, and shows no remorse for his actions. He has been diagnosed by the school psychologist with "Oppositional Defiant Disorder," and his parents are having trouble finding a therapist he likes who will agree to help him with his low self-esteem.

> Karen's parents believe that competition is negative for children, and have guaranteed that all experiences within the family are cooperative and positive, to the point of changing the rules of games so that no one loses. They believe that expressing anger is destructive, and voices are never raised at home. Parental time and attention have no limits. They do not want to be "power parents," since they believe strongly in listening to children's feelings and in focusing on children's needs above and beyond their own.

Karen is ten, and has not been to school for over four months. She has been diagnosed by a psychiatrist with a "Generalized Anxiety Disorder," and has been placed on an anti-anxiety medication usually used for adults.

The syndrome

Although all of these youngsters are presenting quite different issues, they and their parents have much in common. Pushed to an extreme, what starts out as an acceptable parenting philosophy, if left unchecked and unbalanced, can result in entrenched messages and maladaptive behaviors. When the presence of a large number of the following parent characteristics and child behaviors come together and result in a serious family problem requiring intervention, a behavioral disorder that disrupts a child's education or social acceptance, or a psychiatric diagnosis for the child, the Pampered Child Syndrome is born.

Parental characteristics:

- They are striving to be good parents and are willing to do whatever they can to make sure their children are happy and comfortable.

- They are caring, well-meaning, and devoted to their children.

- They have deliberately chosen child-centered parenting philosophies which they believe are designed to maximize their children's well-being and self-esteem.

- They believe that imposing behavioral restrictions interferes with a child's natural development and self-esteem, and feel guilty for doing so.

- They believe in a child's right to make his or her own decisions and choices.

- They provide endless time, money, effort, support, and whatever else they believe makes them a good parent.

- They do not impose their authority because they believe it is inappropriate to do so.

- They try to avoid making children feel upset, embarrassed, or guilty.

- They find it difficult or impossible to say no.

- They are desperately worried about their child's mental well-being, and actively strive to restore their children's happiness and comfort.

Child behaviors:

- They have an exaggerated sense of entitlement and high expectations of service from everyone around them.

- They have low tolerance for discomfort, especially that caused by frustration, disappointment, boredom, delay, and being denied what they want; this is frequently expressed with tantrums, rages, verbal abuse, and/or violence.

- They have developed few, if any, problem-solving resources for dealing with negative experiences.

- They are very self-focused, and believe that they are the center of their world.

- They externalize the reasons for their behaviors, blame everyone else, and expect others to "fix" the problem for them.

- They are unable or unwilling to see how their behaviors affect others, and often lack empathy.

- They sometimes have difficulty feeling guilt or remorse for their behaviors.

- They demand attention, not just from parents, but from everyone. The more they are given, the more they require.

- They have difficulty adapting to the demands of situations outside the family, especially school, since they do not respond well to established social structures or recognized authority figures.

- They are chronically miserable, angry, anxious, and/or emotionally fragile, and frequently have poor self-esteem.

- They meet criteria for a major behavioral or mental disorder, although there is no observable or measurable biological, physiological, developmental, genetic, or other apparently intrinsic reason for their difficulties.

In many instances, these children are difficult to like. They have difficulties with peers when their friends begin to sense that they are expected to pander to their every whim, and social isolation or rejection may be one of the consequences. It is certainly not pleasant for patrons of restaurants, movie theaters, museums, shopping malls, churches, and other public places to be exposed to the uncontrolled behavior of someone else's pampered child. Efforts by various authority figures, such as crossing guards, security personnel, school bus drivers, and so on, are not only not appreciated by the parents, but frequently sabotaged and occasionally actively thwarted. Children who have never been permitted to experience negative feelings, such as guilt or disappointment, have a very hard time empathizing with others' pain or loss, and simply fail to connect to the child whose toy they have broken, the adult whose boundaries they have crossed, or the community whose property they have abused or destroyed.

Recent innovative research is pointed in the direction of confirming a behavior-to-biochemistry connection, in addition to the biochemistry-to-behavior link already in the process of being understood. In other words, we know that certain biochemical patterns in our body produce fairly predictable behaviors. Our hormones and our neurotransmitters work together to affect our moods and our responses to different situations in our environment. A shot of adrenaline will produce a flight, fight, or freeze response. Monthly hormonal cycles will be related to feelings of sexuality and changes in mood. We will experience naturally fluctuating levels of energy, hunger, satisfaction, aggression, relaxation, and so on. Although proposed many decades ago by psychologist Donald Hebb at McGill University,[1] it has taken a long time for acceptance of the notion that behaviors set up their own unique neural pathways and hence a recognizable biochemical pattern that becomes more easily accessible with time and repetition. Thus, if we keep on responding in a given way, while initially voluntary, the behavior pattern may become automatic, and the accompanying biochemical configuration may form part of our basic brain functioning. If it keeps on behaving like a duck, it may eventually be indistinguishable from a duck.

It is important to intervene in the behavioral pattern before it becomes part of nature, rather than nurture, not simply for common-sense, mental well-being, and humanitarian reasons. From a political and economic viewpoint, these pampered children are taking precious education and health care resources away from the youngsters who have legitimate mental health problems that need to be addressed within the shrinking funding available. It is therefore vital to be able to determine which children are truly suffering from the various emotional and behavioral disorders in order to ensure that causal factors are identified and addressed, so that appropriate treatment can be planned. Early identification is the key to ensuring that predictable behavioral patterns are recognized and modified before behavior becomes biochemistry, so that the ounce of prevention can be instigated, before the pound of cure is necessary.

The next few chapters will examine genuine psychological/psychiatric diagnoses that are becoming increasingly common among children and adolescents. We shall look at each one in the light of the Pampered Child Syndrome, and see how difficult and confusing it is to try to separate them – but how important it is to ensure that we do.

Note

1. Hebb, D. (1949) *The Organization of Behavior.* New York: Wiley.

4

Depression

If an accurate differentiation is to be made between a true depressive disorder and the results of too much indulgence, it is necessary to examine the acceptable criteria for diagnosis for the former and compare them with the behavioral patterns of an overly pampered child.

We encountered Jeff briefly at the beginning of Chapter 3. He has been sent by his parents and his family physician for therapy to help him deal with his depression, for which he has been prescribed daily medication. He says that he doesn't really feel any better since he started taking the pills; in fact, nothing really bothers him any more. He has one more semester to complete in order to graduate high school, but has done poorly in his recent exams, and his teachers have all sent home letters of concern. He can't see the point of studying history ("What use is learning about dead people?") or math ("I have no use for math in my life") or science ("It's boring"). When he does make it to school, he spends most of his time in the smoking area with his friends. When he's at home, he's miserable. His dad has recently bought him a drum set to try to cheer him up, because he says he wants to start a band with a couple of the guys. The guitar his parents had given him before was not the type he wanted, and anyway he got bored with the lessons. He says his friend has written some really cool, alternative music, and some guy has promised him the band can cut a CD, but he doesn't have time to practice while he has to go to stupid classes. He admits to smoking marijuana several times a week, but says that his doctor has told him that it's not really harmful. He doesn't drink any more than any of his friends, and stops before he throws up. He complains that his parents are threatening to take away his allowance, although they never do, and that they are always on his case about doing more around the house. He says he doesn't see why he should have to; the cleaning lady comes every week, and his older sisters have now left home, so it's not fair that he should have to pick up all the chores they used to do. He stays up late on the computer, goes to sleep around 3 or 4 A.M. and cannot get himself out of bed in the mornings. He seldom eats at home any more, preferring instead to fill up on beer and cigarettes. His new friends are older, and a few of them have their own apartments, so he's working on his parents to give him some money so he can move out when he turns 18. He's not sure his dad will go for it, but his mom is weakening; she always does, he says, especially when he says he might as well be dead if he's stuck with them forever. He lost his temper with a teacher at school a couple of weeks ago, but he can't see what the big deal is; he punched the wall, not her, he says.

His parents admit to having "spoiled" Jeff. "I know we shouldn't," says his mother, "but we're so much better off now than we've ever been, and it's so wonderful to see him smile when we give him things." They have supported every interest he has ever shown, from music lessons to snowboarding to electronic gadgets, although he never seemed to stick with anything for very long. Now they're starting to expect him to finance his own activities, which Jeff finds totally unfair. They even expect him to pay for gas and insurance for the car. How's he supposed to do that, and have a life? Jeff says his parents made him go to the doctor because they're worried about him. The doctor had him and his parents answer a stupid questionnaire, and the doctor says the results say he's depressed. Whatever. At least his mom has stopped being on his case about going to school, and doesn't ask him to do stuff around the house any more.

In addition to clinical interview and history-taking, the most common tools used in the diagnosis of depression are checklists that ask the child and/or significant adults to rate symptoms in terms of their degree of severity (not at all, just a little, pretty much, very much) and/or frequency of occurrence (never, rarely, sometimes, often). It is not unusual for pampered children like Jeff to score in the mildly to moderately depressed range on such scales, especially if they want to, and it is therefore necessary for the astute parent and clinician-diagnostician to probe a little more deeply to ascertain the context within which each symptom occurs. While there are a number of alternative diagnostic systems, and even different definitions for what constitutes a range of disorders, there are a number of major features that appear to be common to all,[1] so the criteria used here are taken from a number of sources.

Symptom	Depressed child	Pampered child
Negative mood	Usually pervasive, regardless of activity	Present when child is asked to do something he does not like to do
Self-report of sad feelings or hopelessness	Again pervasive; characterized by inability to see way out	Usually situational; child sees solution as adult changing expectations
Irritability or anger	Can be touched off by very, very small issues, even when engaging in positive activities	Evident when denied desired activities, when told "no," when asked to do something child does not want to do. Not present when engaging in desired activities
Changes in appetite; failure to obtain normal weight gain; or excessive weight gain	Usually present in moderate to severe depression, over a period of time	Child may refuse to eat something he/she does not like in an attempt to be provided with alternatives
Changes in activity level – agitation or slowing down	Generalized behavior over a period of time, or may be associated with ongoing mood swings	Present when child does not want to take part in an activity; then may be slow as means of avoidance
Fatigue or tremendous loss of energy	Pervasive, not associated with any activity in particular; child simply cannot energize to do anything	Not usually a feature, unless associated with lack of sleep
Feelings of guilt	Self-blame, self-recrimination quite common	Not usually a feature; child rarely experiences or reports guilt
Low self-esteem	Common and pervasive	Sometimes. However, child may have high opinion of him/herself

Symptom	Depressed child	Pampered child
Poor concentration or forgetfulness	Common and pervasive	Child will attend, concentrate, and remember selectively, e.g., forgets homework but not social events
Suicidal ideation or suicide attempts	If present, usually related to perception of loss, and feelings of helplessness/ hopelessness	If present, often used as lever or threat to get his/her way; may be only issue to elicit parental limits
Changes in school performance	Common; may be sudden or occur over time	If present, usually associated with certain teachers; will work for those he/she likes, not for others
Social avoidance or withdrawal	Common; self-initiated	Usually result of avoidance by peers because of self-focus
Somatic complaints (e.g., headaches, stomach aches)	Common; may result in recognition of underlying "pain"	Uncommon, unless they serve a conscious purpose
Social skills deficits	Result of withdrawal, low affect, irritability; seen as "out of character"	Resulting from lack of empathy, inability to share or take turns, needs to be center of attention
Negative self-statements or negative self-reinforcements	Usually present and evident in general conversation	Rare; usually blames others for his/her misfortunes

Treatment of all forms of depression usually involves medication, along with some form of psychotherapy. Outcome data indicate that the most effective is a combination of both types of intervention; however, these studies have been conducted on adult populations, rather than with children.[2] While there is a range of medications available and effective for adults, the long-term impact of these medications on children is essentially unfolding. At the time of writing, two major medications (Paxil and Effexor) that have been widely used with children and adolescents are now banned because of the increased likelihood of suicidal behaviors and induced manic episodes.[3] There will always be some inherent risk in introducing substances that replace, replicate, or re-uptake naturally occurring neurotransmitters in systems that are still evolving, even if those systems are indeed malfunctioning and not producing the right biochemical balance themselves. There is even more concern with respect to the potential harm that can be inflicted on a young brain that would otherwise have evolved normally, given that the observed "symptoms" can be attributed to behavioral, rather than biological, causes. There is no doubt that appropriate and carefully monitored medical treatment can be enormously effective. Nonetheless, it is important for us, as parents, to remain benignly skeptical with respect to psychotropic medication for our children, ensuring that we are informed consumers who demand reliable and valid data to justify such an approach, even (or perhaps especially) if we are desperate enough to try anything.

In many cases, both depressed *and* pampered children can become suicidal, for different reasons. For the depressed individual, it is most often associated with helplessness, hopelessness, and real or perceived loss. For the pampered child, it is more likely to be triggered by failure of the normal range of levers and manipulative strategies, creating an escalation of demands. Whatever the reason, it is always critical to check out directly and immediately any suggestion or threat, however remote, of self-harm, harm to others, or self-destructive behavior. There is a temptation to perceive suicidal thoughts or gestures, particularly repeated instances, as "attention seeking," which they frequently may be. However, even if they are blatantly self-serving, there is a huge risk in dismissing them out of hand. A youngster who has poor impulse control and who is focused on immediate gratification of needs may well misjudge the severity of what was intended to be a suicidal threat or gesture, and end up dying unintentionally. In situations where parents are working to regain some control over the family and to provide some security in the form of boundaries or limits, pampered children can sometimes resort to extreme measures in an attempt to restore the former status quo. They will hold parents hostage with thinly veiled threats. "There's no point in being here if you won't let me…" Sometimes, the threats are not subtle. "If you won't give me…, I might as well be dead." "If you make me…, I'll kill myself."

It is vitally important for parents to muster the confidence to deal directly with children in this type of situation. We need to understand that, by asking for clarification and/or more information in a supportive environment, we are not going to push a child into killing him or herself. We need to reassure our child that we will indeed act decisively if we sense any threat to his safety. In most cases, this entails a trip to the local emergency room and an extremely lengthy wait. Suicidal children not in immediate danger are not a priority in most hospitals or clinics, and are sometimes treated with some reluctance. They will eventually be seen by a mental health worker or emergency room physician/resident, perhaps followed by a referral to psychiatry or social work, but quite likely by a return trip home with a list of community mental health resources, most or all of which have lengthy waiting lists. Because they know this will be the outcome, perhaps from previous experience, many parents feel that there is no point in following this course of action, particularly because their teenager is unlikely to be cooperative with this plan.

Whether or not we are dealing with a truly depressed or a pampered child, it is important to send the consistent message that threats to life will *always* be taken seriously and acted upon. Thus, we will double-check that this is indeed what the child is intending. This takes guts and the willingness to hear the answers to our questions. "Do you really mean that you would rather be dead?" "Is that what you're really saying – that you'll kill yourself if we don't let you go to the party?" We may also help a child out by offering some viable alternatives. "When you say you'd rather be dead, do you mean that you're really upset about…?" "When you say no one would miss you if you weren't around, it sounds to me as if you're feeling ignored…" If the child concurs, we have opened a new avenue for discussion. We can then assure the child that we know he is quite able to use different words to express what he is thinking or feeling, and therefore this is what he is expected to do in the future. We can then also assure him that, should we hear another life-threatening statement, we will assume that he means it, and off to the hospital we shall go. Yes, again. And again.

A child who is using suicidal threats to get what he wants will only continue to do so if they work. We must therefore be vigilant to ensure that they never, ever work. It is also important that we make the youngster very aware of the emotional impact of such threats, and use the opportunity to teach a very important lesson in empathy. We need at some point to explain to a young teenager who is using this emotional blackmail that the notion of her dying or being permanently damaged is incredibly distressing for others, as well as whatever is precipitating it must obviously be for her. In many years of experience working with depressed and suicidal individuals, the reason I have most often heard for not taking the final, lethal step has been "I would, but I know how much it would upset my mom/dad/children/best friend…" If we didn't know this, what *would* stop us?

Of course, not all depressed individuals become suicidal. And not all are truly "depressed." True depressive symptoms are chronic, lasting at least six months, and affecting an individual's basic physiological functioning – eating, sleeping, energy, sex drive, and general activity levels. With our children, in particular, we need to encourage them to substitute other words for "depressed," those that match their feelings, so that we can see what we are actually dealing with. Sad, disappointed, discouraged, down, tired, worried, rejected, lonely, fearful, overwhelmed – all very legitimate feelings, all normal, all inevitable at times, and all feelings with which we can empathize and for which we can often find the cause and provide support. But none with the immediate connotation of "mental illness" conjured up by the term "depression."

Pampered children, like all others, will experience the whole range of these different, unpleasant feelings. Learning to identify, differentiate, and label them is an essential first step, for us as well as for our children. Learning to stay with our feelings, experience them, and tolerate them is also important, as is the vital understanding that we do not always have to act on them. If we believe we do, recognizing that each feeling heads off in a different direction for resolution is yet another step. Then we can perhaps help our children by teaching them various ways of addressing the underlying issues and *dealing* with the feelings, rather than creating a non-existent, fantasy world for them, where unpleasantness is to be avoided at all costs.

Notes

1. Dudley, C.D. (1997) *Treating Depressed Children.* Oakland, CA: New Harbinger Publications Inc.

2. Mash, E.J. and Barkley, R.A. (1989) *Treatment of Childhood Disorders.* New York/London: The Guilford Press.

3. Kluger, J. (2004) "Medicating Young Minds." *Time Magazine (Canadian Edition).* 19 January.

5

Anxiety

Pampered children who develop high levels of anxiety are in some respects different from most of the other youngsters we are encountering while discussing the Pampered Child Syndrome. They are usually not so obviously demanding, nor so overtly "entitled." They control us, not by flagrantly challenging our authority, nor by being in-our-faces defiant, but by much more passive, indirect means. They are most often brought to the attention of various professionals for such issues as: school refusal; social withdrawal; difficulties with getting to sleep or staying asleep; bedwetting; stress-related illnesses; and sometimes more serious phobias, such as a fear of leaving the house.

> Karen had been diagnosed with a Generalized Anxiety Disorder by a child psychiatrist at the local hospital. She was ten years old, and her family had relocated to her current home the previous summer because of her dad's job. Prior to the move, she had been educated in a small private school with an educational philosophy that allowed children to learn what they wanted to learn when they wanted to learn it, and to progress at their own pace. Because she was a bright little girl, she had never had any difficulties academically, and her parents had been delighted with her love of music, art, and literature. Because they could not find a similar setting for her after they moved, her parents decided to place her in the local village school in Grade 5 so that she would be able to find friends in the neighborhood and walk to and from school with her little brother. This had been a disaster almost from the beginning. They reported that she initially seemed to be very excited about the move and the new school, but that things began to fall apart

very quickly. By the third week of September, they were having a great deal of difficulty persuading her to get ready in the mornings. Into October and November, she had developed significant headaches, a suspected stomach ulcer, and a sleep disorder. By the beginning of March, she had missed four full months of school, and her mother had been trying valiantly to keep her up to date with her classroom work, with the help of an occasional visit from an itinerant teacher. Karen was begging to be homeschooled and her parents were seeking some advice.

In the course of providing background information, they talked about their own histories, home life, parenting philosophies, and aspirations for their children. They were both the products of very rigid parents who had authoritarian, even marginally abusive, approaches to child-rearing, so they had made a conscious decision to make their home as nurturing, safe, and protective as possible. They maintained that no one in their home ever got angry and that there was no conflict in their marriage. Karen and her brother got along just wonderfully all the time. They parented by consensus, and by debating and negotiating issues until a satisfactory resolution could be reached. They had regular family meetings, and they were all very practiced at talking so others would listen, and listening so others would talk. They believed in collaboration, not competition, and had tried to ensure that all games played in the house were cooperative. Those that were not had been changed to ensure that they were, so that no one ever lost and all victories were shared. There were no computer games, video games, television, or Internet access, and all reading materials were carefully screened to make certain that the subject matter was consistent with their family values. The children's friends all came from "nice families," primarily those they had met through their church.

Karen's parents were distressed by their daughter's obvious unhappiness and wanted to do something to make her feel better, although they were not sure they wanted to follow the psychiatrist's recommendation for medication. They had tried desperately to explain to the school that Karen required a kinder, more flexible approach, and that something needed to be done about the way the other children were so noisy, competitive, and just plain mean. The classroom teacher simply was not concerned, they said, but rather insisted that this was just girls being girls and boys being boys. They were waiting for a meeting with the principal, but didn't hold out much hope for change. They were considering moving back to where they came from, even though this would mean a significant sacrifice for the rest of the family. But they would do anything for Karen.

One of the hardest things for us to do as parents is to see our children suffer. It is a natural instinct for most of us to protect them from harm of any kind, and to try to change the cruel world so that they do not have to endure hardship. We take them into our beds so that they will be safe from the monsters under their own. And we try to come up with a range of alternative routes to avoid the troll under the bridge. By the time they leave this lovely, safe environment, we have laid some firm foundations for the messages that they are very special, and that the world is a safe, nurturing environment.

The cold shower of reality hits at different points for different children. Sometimes this occurs when they first venture outside their own family – to a babysitter's, to daycare, to nursery school, to a friend's house. Sometimes parents work hard to ensure that such experiences are carefully planned so that one safe, nurturing environment is simply seamlessly replaced by another, and the transition is completed with blissful ignorance of the change. Thus, children like Karen can remain cocooned from harsh reality for many years.

The trauma of no longer being special can be devastating for many youngsters. As with any other stress, they may react with a fight, flight, or freeze reaction – tackling the challenges head on, running away and hiding, or becoming paralyzed and unable to move. It is important to understand which of these alternative responses is a child's normal reaction, as well as to understand patterns of anxiety management within families, if we are to deal with pampered children who become anxious when the pampering is unavailable.

As with depression, a combination of medication and psychotherapy is often recommended for anxiety disorders, and the same caveats apply. Most often, in practice, and especially with younger children, behavioral interventions can be extraordinarily effective – provided parents, teachers, and significant others are on board with the mission statement, which is to teach the child to become more resilient in the face of stress, and to develop the ability to self-soothe during episodes of anxiety. If the adults in a child's life believe that it is their obligation to prevent a child from ever being stressed or anxious, and that it is their duty to provide external comfort at all times, the row is exceptionally hard to hoe. The world outside the family is often stressful and anxiety-provoking, despite every effort to make it less so, since stressors are often quite difficult to predict. For example, some children may be more stressed by what seems to others to be a petty disagreement with a friend, than they are by major family transitions. Double messages (e.g., saying one thing, doing another) may provoke high levels of anxiety. Family breakdown is arguably the biggest stressor for children of any age, and yet most divorcing parents will argue that children are better off with a separation than they would be staying in an unhappy environment – a position questioned by recent, longitudinal research.[1]

Children who have been well protected from the real world, where unfair practices prevail, and where survival of the fittest is the rule of the day, will frequently crumble when confronted with the "jungle" of the classroom or schoolyard. Peers are not willing to defer to one's every whim, nor to tolerate *prima donna* behavior, nor to be treated like servants or second-class citizens. Conflict is there to be faced, not avoided, and favoritism runs rampant.

If, therefore, we are to help children like Karen, we must be prepared to take baby steps on the road to resilience. Home is where this process has its roots. It is helpful to provide a home atmosphere that allows children to train for real life. We need to be aware of this when we are unwittingly reinforcing our children's anxieties. When we take a child into our bed because she is frightened of something in her own room, we are telling her we agree with her that there is something to be frightened about. This does not mean that we throw her into her darkened room, lock the door, and throw away the key. Not at all. But it does mean that we are going to support and reinforce her for facing her fears and thus diminishing them, rather than throw fuel on the fire.

We also need to set clear and consistent boundaries. Children are far more reassured and secure when they know that the consequence they have chosen actually occurs. "If you push Button A, this will happen; if you push Button B, that will happen." We explain to them what each choice entails, and ensure that they understand. However much we may warn them not to push B because the consequence is negative, and however much we may coach them to push A, if they choose B, they choose B, and the negative consequence will indeed be forthcoming. This breeds safety and trust.

Saying what we mean and meaning what we say are two very powerful interventions to prevent or address anxiety. Understanding leads to prediction; prediction leads to control. If a parent says one thing, but does another, confusion reigns. If he or she is consistent, even if what they say they will do is unpleasant or negative, at least a child is able to predict what is coming, and learn to act accordingly. If a parent gets drunk every Friday night, comes home, and becomes abusive, a child can begin to predict the pattern and plan what to do about it.

Competition, at least against oneself, is necessary if we are to progress. If we don't care about doing a little better or a little more than we did the previous time, we will stagnate. The little league team that gives all players the Most Valuable Player award will stifle ambition, drive, and motivation. What's the point in trying, if you get the medal anyhow? Yes, in a more competitive system, it is tough for the child who never wins the medals or the prizes. However, only one person will win the promotion, or get the scholarship, or have the choice shift, so we need to learn early on in life to deal with this. Motivation does not arise from comfort, but from discomfort.

Teaching self-soothing behaviors is an important contribution that parents can make to their children's ability to handle anxiety and stress. Rather than relying solely on Mom or Dad for comfort or support, each child needs to accumulate a range of strategies to settle themselves down in moments of stress and anxiety. If his only strategy is to "seek Mom," then he will be at a loss whenever Mom is not around. Even quite young babies can learn to rely on themselves in times of anxiety, such as when they waken in the night. Some children suck their thumb from prenatal times; others hum to themselves, or hold on to stuffed animals or blankets. If we are to wean our children from total reliance on us, we need to ensure that we can replace ourselves with some transitional object (a piece of our clothing, a toy we have given, a photograph of ourselves) that can serve as a security "bridge" and provide a virtual reality experience. We have to act with conviction when replacing ourselves with plastic, fuzzy, or paper replicas. We also have to prove to our children that we shall indeed return.

There is little doubt that anxiety is hereditary – or at least runs in families for whatever reasons. The biggest barrier to a child's ability to overcome anxiety is frequently the parent or parents who also carry this burden. If we transmit the message that we believe the world is an unsafe place, our children will not venture out into it; moreover, we will not let them go. We must teach our children to negotiate the bumps in the road, and then trust them to do so.

Note

1. Wallerstein, J.S., Lewis, J.M. and Blakeslee, S. (2000) *The Unexpected Legacy of Divorce: The 25 Year Landmark Study.* New York: Hyperion.

6

Attention Deficit Hyperactive Disorder

The concept of Attention Deficit Hyperactive Disorder (ADHD) has been around for just over a century, encompassing symptoms and signs related to inattention, impulsivity, and over-activity, with the resulting behavioral and learning difficulties. The diagnostic label has undergone many metamorphoses along the way, reflecting the evolving beliefs of the times. It began as a "defect in moral control" and "volitional inhibition,"[1] later became the "Strauss Syndrome" and "Minimal Brain Dysfunction,"[2] and subsequently "Hyperkinetic Reaction of Childhood"[3] in the late 1960s. Recognition that there was more to it than over-activity led to a number of shifts through various labels[4] to the present-day ADHD, with various recognizable subtypes (e.g., Restless/ Impulsive, Inattentive, Hyperactive),[5] ADHD is currently accepted as a neuro- logically based, rather than a behaviorally based, disorder, that is widely treated with medications such as Ritalin, Concerta, Dexedrine, and so on, and for which parental training in appropriate behavior management techniques is an important adjunct.

An emerging view of the same cluster of behaviors and characteristics postulates a "Disorder of Self Regulation"[6] which takes account of the fact that these children can become overly focused, as well as exhibiting a short attention span and distractibility, depending on circumstances. The whole notion of self-regulation, of course, requires investigation into whether a child is not only *capable* of controlling his impulses and maintaining his attention, but also whether he *chooses* to. Children are not born being able to discipline themselves; self-discipline arises from years of training, and is, according to child development specialists, a "gift" to children from their parents.[7]

It is not, therefore, surprising that many pampered children, who have not been taught to wait, to persevere in the face of challenges, or to focus their attention, end up being misdiagnosed as having ADHD.

> Angela, aged six, is referred for assessment toward the second half of her Grade I year because she has recently been diagnosed as having an Attention Deficit Hyperactive Disorder and placed on Ritalin, and her parents are asking for suggestions to help with her learning. She is the only child of their relationship, although both parents each have two older adolescent children from former marriages who spend considerable time in their home and who love Angie to distraction. Laughing, they say that she has "six servants!" They themselves are both experienced parents who figure that they can simply leave her be, and her development will just "unfold" as it did with their other children. They describe her as vivacious, affectionate, and a free spirit, with a wonderfully creative imagination and mature language skills, whose bubbly nature is a delight to them both.
>
> It has come as a major shock at the recent parent/teacher interview to be told that Angie is in danger of being retained in Grade I because she is having great difficulty with her academics. Her teacher says that she is not paying attention in class, can't sit still for circle time, loses things she needs, doesn't finish what she starts, and is having great difficulty acquiring basic skills, claiming that everything is "boring." She clearly does not enjoy printing, and prefers to be read to, rather than try to read for herself. The teacher had given them the name of a pediatrician to whom the school frequently referred children they suspected of having ADHD, and suggested they might want to have her assessed. They had filled in a number of forms, the doctor had spent five minutes with Angie, and they had come away with a prescription. Angie, of course, had not been on her best behavior that day, and made a bit of a mess of the waiting room and the doctor's office. They have read the literature he gave them, and really feel that she fits the description to a T. They started her on the medication a few weeks ago, but they have observed a negative change in her sunny nature, and her teacher is still complaining that her work is not being done.
>
> A thorough psychological assessment, conducted off medication, shows that Angie is a child with high-average abilities and no evidence

of any attention or learning problems. Her listening attention and memory are above age level, as are her visual attention and memory skills. Tedious, repetitive tasks are completed accurately, even though she protests loudly at having to do them. There are no language difficulties that might be impinging on her ability to learn, nor are there any signs of non-verbal deficits or pattern recognition problems that would lead to difficulties acquiring academic skills. Standardized rating scales obtained from both her parents and her teacher, however, clearly place her at clinically significant levels on diagnostic measures of ADHD: Inattentive Type. Despite these ratings and the fact that Angie is doing poorly in Grade 1, there is a reluctance on the part of the psychologist to make a diagnosis because of her own observations, and because of the lack of support for inattentiveness in the individual cognitive assessment data. The parents are now stuck between the medical and psychological points of view.

Further exploration is required here to see how a pampered child, who has not been taught to wait, to follow through, to pay attention to detail, or to be seen but not heard under certain circumstances, can reach diagnostic criteria for ADHD: Inattentive Type. In order to do so, we shall examine some of the behaviors that are frequently included on standardized rating scales measuring various aspects of attention, such as the Conners' Rating Scales which has a version for both parents and teachers.[8]

On most rating scales, behaviors are scored on a scale ranging from "never or seldom" through "occasionally" and "often" to "very frequently." To reach significance, a child must score at or above a criterion level that places him or her at the 98th percentile compared to other children of the same age and gender. It is of interest to note that six-year-old boys who score the same number of absolute points as their female age-peers on such scales are often considered to be within normal limits for their age, whereas the girls may well reach criterion for diagnosis. In other words, little boys are expected to be intrinsically less attentive than their female counterparts! Usually, both parents are asked to complete separate ratings, as are the child's teachers, since an ADHD diagnosis requires the symptoms to be consistently present in more than one major area of the child's life.

The responses to the following questions show how some of the behaviors commonly noted in children with attention problems may be perceived differently by parents and teachers, yet rated fairly comparably.

"Avoids, expresses reluctance about, or has difficulties engaging in tasks that require sustained mental effort (such as schoolwork or homework)"[8]

Parents' response: Often. Angie's parents report that she is a very sensitive youngster, who cries when "pressured," so they make every attempt not to pressure her. And they don't like it when she is unhappy or uncomfortable. One or other of them will sit with her to do her homework, and when she has had enough, or when it becomes too hard for her, they let her go and play, because they don't believe that children of this age should be given work to do at home. She needs to have time to play and be a child, doesn't she?

Teachers' response: Very often. Her teacher says that Angie will do everything she can to avoid doing anything that she sees as "work." Her avoidance repertoire is impressive, and includes: chatting with other children, "helping" others, needing to go to the washroom frequently, saying that the work is "too hard," crying.

"Has difficulty sustaining attention in tasks or play activities"[8]

Parents' response: Often. Her parents describe her as a very extroverted youngster, who likes change and who gets bored easily. Mom comments that they actually encourage Angie to engage in lots of different activities, because they don't want her to become too narrow in her interests, like one of her other children who is too focused on his girlfriend. She has inherited many toys and games from her older half-siblings, a couple of whom battle with each other over who gets to play with her, and who are constantly tempting her with new activities.

Teachers' response: Very often. In class, Angie flits from one activity center to another, needing to be reminded that she is supposed to finish the activity and then tidy up before moving on. The teacher has noticed the same tendency at recess, where Angie will play with some children for a very short while before going off to join another group of friends.

"Does not seem to listen to what is being said to him/her"[8]

Parents' response: Occasionally. Dad says that he doesn't have much difficulty getting Angie to listen to him, but Mom seems to struggle with this on occasion. Angie tends to tune Mom out when she's being asked to stop doing something she enjoys, and/or when she is asked to initiate an activity she doesn't like doing. She seems to listen fine when being offered something pleasurable.

Teachers' response: Often. Both her classroom teacher and her French teacher comment that Angie often seems to be in a world of her own, or chatting with her neighbor, and that they frequently have to say her name and repeat what they have said in order to ensure that she has listened. It is hard for them to say whether her listening is selective, since they are mostly asking her to get on with her work.

> "Does not follow through on instructions and fails to finish school work (not due to oppositional behavior or failure to understand instructions)"[8]

Parents' response: Often. Both parents admit that it is hard to get Angie to finish what she starts, or to get her to do what they ask her to do. She procrastinates and procrastinates, until they end up doing it for her. "It's just easier," they both say. "We're often in too much of a hurry to wait."

Teachers' response: Very often. Her classroom teacher says that she doesn't think it's oppositional behavior, because Angie is such a pleasant, polite, but somewhat immature little girl. She just sees her as not really focusing on what has been said, and being more interested in playing than working.

> "Has difficulty organizing tasks or activities"[8]

Parents' response: Occasionally. Most of the time at home, Angie is fairly bossy, and gets everyone else to organize things for her, which they do to keep the peace. But she seems to know what it is she wants and how she wants it!

Teachers' response: Very often. In the classroom, Angie seems very "scattered," according to her teacher. She can't seem to get things together to get on with her various activities, and looks to others to do it for her. "It's as if she's used to having servants," her teacher comments.

> "Fails to give close attention to detail or makes careless mistakes in schoolwork, work, or other activities"[8]

Parents' response: Very often. Because she is so creative and is always following new ideas, both parents agree that Angie is a "big picture person" for whom details are not important. "She's just like me," confesses her mother. "I can't bear having to dot the 'I's and cross the 'T's!" They notice that she does not like to check over her homework to see if she's done it correctly, and is very reluctant to change what she has written or drawn if they point out to her that there are some errors.

Teachers' response: Very often. Like her parents, both her classroom teacher and her French teacher have remarked on her grasp of overall concepts, but her reluctance to polish up her work. She is definitely not a perfectionist, and therefore is not fazed by mistakes. "My mom says it doesn't matter if it's not perfect," she insists.

"Forgetful in daily activities"[8]
"Forgets things he/she has already learned"[8]

Parents' response: Occasionally. Her parents do not generally see her as forgetful, commenting that she's only six and that they are not concerned if she forgets things once in a while.

Teachers' response: Often. There is certainly some concern at school over her difficulties with the acquisition of early reading and writing skills, and her teacher feels that there may be some memory difficulties. She seems to know how to print her alphabet accurately on some occasions, but makes mistakes on others, sometimes missing a letter, or reversing her "b"s and "d"s, even though they have gone over and over this in class and for homework. Her teacher knows that the parents do not make her practice at home, and feels this may have something to do with it.

"Loses things necessary for tasks or activities (e.g., school assignments, pencils, books, tools, or toys)"[8]

Parents' response: Occasionally. It's not so much that Angie loses things, say her parents. It's that she can't be bothered to find them! They usually end up finding them for her, because if they don't, she won't care enough to carry through with the activity, and will simply go do something else.

Teachers' response: Often. Her teacher believes this to be related to Angie's difficulties organizing herself. She certainly is frequently unprepared for activities, even when they involve things she likes to do.

"Easily distracted by extraneous stimuli"[8]

Parents' response: Very often. Again, her parents reiterate that Angie is an extrovert with a large number of interests who is very easily bored. She is also very curious about things, and likes to be in the midst of whatever is going on. They value her observation skills, and the way she notices everything around her. They believe that this is a strength, and that she will manage this better as she gets older.

Teachers' response: Very often. Her teacher comments that Angie is a very active learner, paying attention to many things both within and outside the classroom. She sees this getting in the way of her focusing on important and relevant learning issues, and says it wouldn't be such a problem if only Angie could be more easily redirected to paying attention.

Despite the fact that Angie's parents and teachers have somewhat different interpretations of the same behavioral label, and the fact that their ratings are often slightly discrepant, Angie would, in fact, meet the criteria for significance on the Conners' ADHD: Inattentive Type scale, which could well be the justification for both a diagnosis and potentially for medical treatment. While practitioners who are experienced with the multi-disciplinary approach to ADHD would not rely solely on a single objective measure for a diagnosis, there is sometimes an unfortunate tendency to utilize the results from an abbreviated test battery in order to support a subjective judgment and/or to pressure parents into utilizing medication to tackle troublesome symptoms.

Angie's behaviors are quite definitely affecting her ability to adapt to the more structured environment of school, and are likely to interfere to a high degree with her ability to learn, especially when she is not intrinsically interested in the materials being presented. And yet they are quite consistent with her parents' philosophies and the messages they are sending. Unfortunately, it is sometimes not until a child is actually failing quite dramatically that we parents will consider shifting our belief systems to acknowledge that we may, unwittingly, have something to do with this situation. And, even when we do, it is difficult for us to change our behavior so that we can actually tolerate, or even sometimes precipitate, some discomfort in our children so that they will be motivated to change their way of doing things.

None of this discussion of the misdiagnosis of some pampered children is intended to take away from the genuine needs of appropriately diagnosed children with ADHD. There are clearly a number of children who legitimately fit the profile, and who have the underlying neurological-biochemical imbalances that fuel a central nervous system that functions in overdrive, or that creates gaps in attention, or that prevents an individual from filtering out background noise or detail in order to focus on relevant information.

In addition, there is the important note that true ADHD is not *caused* by poor parenting, although there are some parenting strategies that help manage these children somewhat more successfully. It is often, however, considered by parents and professionals alike to be "parent-blaming" if questions are asked or statements made that imply that parents could be contributing to or responsible for a child's inappropriate behavior, and many clinicians try to stay away from this politically sensitive issue. The point remains that, unless professionals, especially those who are qualified to make formal diagnoses, explore parenting philosophies and beliefs, and follow up by assessing the impact of various parenting values and practices on a child's behavior, we may well be over-diagnosing such disorders as ADHD, and, much worse, prescribing medication inappropriately as a means of addressing the problems.

Notes

1. Still, G.F. (1902) "Some abnormal psychical conditions in children." *The Lancet 1*, 1008–1012, 1077–1082, 1163–1168.

2. Strauss, A.A. and Lehtinen, L.E. (1947) *Psychopathology and Education of the Brain-Injured Child*. New York: Grune and Stratton.

3. American Psychiatric Association (1968) *Diagnostic and Statistical Manual. Second Edition (DSM-II)*. Washington, DC: American Psychiatric Association.

4. Barkley, R.A. (1998) "Attention Deficit Disorder with Hyperactivity." In E.J. Mash and L.G. Terdal (eds) *Behavioral Assessment of Childhood Disorders. Second Edition*. New York: The Guilford Press.

5. American Psychiatric Association (1994) *Diagnostic and Statistical Manual. Fourth Edition (DSM-IV)*. Washington, DC: American Psychiatric Association.

6. Barkley, R.A. (2000) *A New Look at ADHD: Inhibition, Time, and Self-Control*. Video. New York: The Guilford Press.

7. Coloroso, B. (1994) *Kids Are Worth It! Giving Your Child the Gift of Inner Discipline*. Toronto, ON: Somerville House.

8. Conners, C.K. (1997) *Conners' Rating Scales – Revised (CRS–R)*. Toronto, ON: Multi-Health Systems Inc. Copyright © 1997 Multi-Health Systems Inc. All rights reserved. In the USA, P.O. Box 950, North Tonawanda, NY 14120-0950, 1-800-456-3003. In Canada, 3770 Victoria Park Ave., Toronto, ON M2H 3M6, 1-800-268-6011. Internationally, +1-416-492-2627. Fax, +1-416-492-3343. Reproduced with permission.

7

Behavior Disorders

Lack of respect for authority is one of the main underlying issues that creates the foundation for both Oppositional Defiant Disorder (ODD) and Conduct Disorder diagnoses. These behaviorally based disorders differ from most other mental health diagnoses in that they do not imply causes that are entirely intrinsic to the individual, but rather that they stem from extrinsic factors, and involve the individual's interactions with his or her environment. In particular, quality of family environment has been linked with the development of both ODD and the more serious Conduct Disorder.[1]

Oppositional Defiant Disorder is characterized by the following ongoing (for six months or more) behaviors, only four of which are required for diagnosis: loses temper; argues with adults; actively defies or refuses to comply with adults' requests or rules; deliberately annoys people; blames others for his or her mistakes or misbehavior; touchy or easily annoyed by others; angry and resentful; spiteful or vindictive. In order to meet criteria, the behavioral disturbance has to be causing significant impairment in social, academic, or occupational functioning, and other disorders need to be ruled out (i.e., Psychotic or Mood Disorder, Conduct Disorder, and Antisocial Personality Disorder for individuals over 18).[2] Once the behaviors become more serious, and involve aggression to people or animals, destruction of property, deceitfulness or theft, and serious rule violation (including running away from home overnight, truancy, etc.), the criteria for a Conduct Disorder are met,[3] and the youngster is more likely to be dealt with through the corrections and justice systems, rather than by mental health professionals.

Since pampered children, by definition, lack respect for authority, albeit often in a benign way, the potential for overlap with these disorders is obvious, especially when youngsters become angry and resentful of adults who interfere with their beliefs about how the world should be treating them. They often begin to get into trouble when they refuse to comply with commands or requests by adults,[4] particularly those outside the family. However, pampered children are usually driven by their sense of entitlement to equality with adults, rather than by the spitefulness and vindictiveness that drives the child with ODD.

Paul's mother, Serena, is desperate to find a therapist who will help her oldest son. She has been told by the school psychologist that they need help before his behaviors escalate even further and he finds himself in trouble with the police. She has taken Paul to three different people already, but he didn't like any of them. "They're all idiots," is his articulate analysis, "and what's more, they treat me like a child!"

She and her ex-husband, Tom, have made a real effort to parent together, even though they have been separated for seven years, just after Paul turned six, and don't like each other much. Tom has been a good dad, despite his former alcoholism, and the fact that he doesn't see Paul that regularly because his son refuses to visit. He loves his children dearly, even if he can't always be there for them. From the beginning, both parents have always expected Paul to make his own decisions, to be self-sufficient, to question everything, and to take initiative whenever possible, especially when he became the "man of the house" after his dad left. He tries hard, but tends to blame his younger brother and sister whenever there is trouble at home. There are very few "rules" at Mom's, because Serena believes that restrictions stifle initiative and erode self-esteem. Dad has some rules, like cleaning up after yourself, but he usually doesn't follow up, and all three children know how to get around him pretty easily. Both Serena and Tom have always deliberately stayed away from telling Paul what is right or wrong because they want him to make up his own mind. Both of them intervene when other adults try to impose their views on him, and defend him rigorously whenever he is criticized. They admire and encourage his ability to stand up for himself, although they recognize that others may not always be as impressed.

Paul has run into a number of problems with teachers over the years – nothing serious, mostly "attitude," and occasionally mouthing off. While he is a very capable student, he works only sporadically, when he sees the point, or when he likes a particular teacher. He respects only those who are willing to provide him with a rationale for why he should invest his energy. Serena is concerned that he has a bad reputation, and that some of the staff are now fingering him for things he doesn't actually do.

It still came as quite a blow when the call came from the principal a few months ago, saying that Paul and one of his friends had been named by a younger student as instigators of some bullying, including intimidation, coercion, and aggressive teasing, allegations which their son indignantly denied. The meeting with the teachers had been distressing, but both Tom and Serena had defended Paul vigorously, and had let the school know that a lawyer was being readied, should this incident be taken any further. They had all finally decided that Paul should see the school psychologist because of how this situation might be related to what his teachers see as his low self-esteem, and Paul agreed, because this was the negotiated alternative to a lengthy suspension. Somewhat to his parents' surprise, Paul appeared to be unmoved by the whole process. He thought the principal was a dork, and that the teachers were just sheep, following blindly along without minds of their own. They had let it go, because they believed him, and besides which no actual harm had been done. Honestly, Tom said, some people are just so over-protective of their children. Boys will be boys, after all! If you can't trust your own children, who can you trust?

There is consensus in the literature that ODD and Conduct Disorder emanate from parenting behaviors that focus on giving significant negative attention to undesirable behavior, especially when dealing with children whose temperament tends to be somewhat difficult and irritable. Positive results have been obtained from interventions that target behavior management issues from the earliest possible age, whether these be parenting skills, school-based programs, and/or mental health agencies.[5]

For pampered children, there is a danger of being labeled with a behavioral diagnosis which can then color the child's reputation for years to come. It is often extremely difficult for us as parents to recognize that our children are behaving in ways that are unacceptable to others outside the family, or perhaps even to extended family members. Being told by a mother-in-law, a brother, an aunt or uncle, or grandparent, that one's children are "spoiled" or "indulged" is worse than a slap in the face. A "friend" who ventures a similar opinion will no longer be counted among our acquaintances. Not only are our precious offspring being criticized, but so are we. We can, and often do, attribute intrafamilial criticism to jealousy, dislike, or simply old-fashioned ideas. But what if we also receive similar input from babysitters, nursery school staff, teachers, coaches, neighbors, bus drivers, and the like? How long can we go on ignoring it, or attributing it all to some vague ulterior motive?

Most of us want our children to be liked and admired by others. So we are clearly not voluntarily intending to put them in a position where they will be actively ignored or rejected by their extended family, peers, and various significant others. There is no question that well-behaved children are accepted everywhere. Thus, our obligation as parents is to ensure that our children behave well, as judged by the society in which they currently happen to live. We delegate some of this responsibility to caregivers and to school personnel, so we need to ensure that our values are reflected in the various environments in which we place our children over the years. One of our biggest headaches is how to help them process and integrate the multitude of other influences and competing value systems they will inevitably encounter, until such time as they approach the end of adolescence and head off into the world of adulthood, bearing total responsibility for their own decisions and choices.

This is all very well, parents say, but we see the enormity of that task, and recognize its impossibility. It is at this point that we must not sigh and give up. We need to have confidence in our ability to effect change in our families, and to persist in living and teaching our value systems, mindful of the necessity of adaptation and change with every successive generation. Our children may turn to their friends for current trends, but they look to us for the deeper values, and we know that, for the most part, they tend to come back to whatever family standards we have consistently lived and modeled. Later, we shall examine more closely the impact that parents and others can have on ensuring the necessary balance for pampered children, so that we can continue to nurture, but also provide guidance and the security of limits on their behavior.

Notes

1. Rey, J.M., Walter, G., Plapp, J.M. and Denshire, E. (2000) "Family environment in attention deficit hyperactivity, oppositional defiant and conduct disorders." *Australian and New Zealand Journal of Psychiatry 34*, (3), 453.

2. Long, P.W. (2003) *Oppositional Defiant Disorder – American Description.* Obtainable from Internet Mental Health. www.mentalhealth.com

3. American Psychiatric Association (1994) *Diagnostic and Statistical Manual. Fourth Edition (DSM-IV)*. Washington, DC: American Psychiatric Association.

4. Tynan, W.D. (2004) *Oppositional Defiant Disorder*. eMedicine.com, Inc.

5. Tynan, W.D. (2004) *Oppositional Defiant Disorder*. eMedicine.com, Inc.

8

Learning Problems

It may come as something of a surprise to find a chapter on learning problems in this book. This is because most of us tend, quite rightly, not to associate learning disabilities with parental goals or messages, or with children's personality or behavioral characteristics, but rather with underlying neurological or neuropsychological difficulties within the central nervous system that affect the ability of the brain to process certain types of information in certain ways. There are, however, a number of situations where the messages that a child has internalized about himself or the world around him can interfere to a significant degree with his ability to be an active learner, to practice various skills, and to solve problems independently, using his full range of cognitive abilities and learning strategies.

Jessica is 13 and in Grade 8. She was diagnosed with a mild learning disability about four years ago when the family was living in British Columbia. While she struggles a little with her reading and her written skills, she apparently has her greatest difficulty in math, to the point where she has developed quite a phobia about it, becoming excessively nervous when she knows she is going to be asked to perform. She is currently barely passing, and her teacher is concerned that her advancement to Grade 9 may be affected. Her parents are asking for a reassessment in order to ascertain the degree of problem, to determine how to help her, to settle on an appropriate high school placement, and for guidance for her in terms of future career directions and a life without math.

Thorough psychological and educational assessments confirm that she is a bright young lady, and reveal no pattern of abilities that is even remotely suggestive of an underlying learning disability. In fact, when Jessica's math skills are formally evaluated, she does not appear to have any major gaps in her basic knowledge, although she requires some prompting to remember the various procedures. It is, however, noted by the educational consultant that Jessica is extremely reluctant to try even the simplest examples, and that she looks for assistance with every question, even though she can actually manage quite well when assistance is refused and she is encouraged to go ahead on her own. When left alone, she seems to run out of power, like a solar-powered calculator does when there is no source of light. She sits and waits until someone comes back. The same passive approach is also evident in some other academic areas that involve the need for active problem solving, such as science, research projects, and so on, and she relies again on adult input to encourage and nudge her through the various tasks.

Further exploration with her parents indicates that Jessica is, in fact, quite a controlling young lady at home! She is very fussy about what she will or won't eat, wear, do, and tolerate. She refuses to do her homework unless she has at least one parent by her side. It is clear that she has at least two servants (her mother and father) who try to satisfy her every whim, but who, according to Jessica, frequently fall short. She apparently has quite a temper, and has regular hissy fits when things do not go her way, or when her parents fail to live up to her expectations for support. They have given up trying to get her to do chores, because it's easier to do them themselves. She has several entrenched beliefs, including: I should never do anything that I don't feel like doing; I should never be uncomfortable, and when I am, someone should do something to make me comfortable again; and I am entitled to the full attention of both my parents at all times. Her mother does not work outside the home, and feels it is her obligation to do everything for her children, since this is, in fact, her job. Mom feels guilty if she asks Jessica to do anything for herself, and so she doesn't. She also feels guilty if she doesn't help with homework, although, as she freely admits, she "doesn't do math" and so her husband is allowed to take the math and science shifts.

As a result, Jessica has become a selective learner and a passive problem solver, relying on adult help to get her through the curriculum, and refusing to tackle any task that she senses is hard. She will learn what she feels like learning, and she will continue to look as if she has a learning disability, mostly because everyone around her expects it of her. Because of her previous identification, she is receiving remedial assistance from the scant resources available, and she will most likely continue to deprive another student with genuine difficulties of the help he or she requires. Both parents are skeptical when it comes to suggestions that they might want to back off and let her use her strong reasoning skills to figure things out for herself, and it is clear that they do not believe she can. They see themselves as having a job for life, and they probably do.

As Mary Pipher has said in *Reviving Ophelia*,[1] a wonderful book about adolescent girls:

> My observations suggest that girls have trouble in math because math requires exactly the qualities that many junior-high girls lack – confidence, trust in one's own judgment and the ability to tolerate frustration without becoming overwhelmed... Girls need to be encouraged to persevere in the face of difficulty, to calm down and believe in themselves.

No wonder pampered children sometimes develop pseudo-learning problems. The dependent learner, who relies on, and receives, direction and constant bolstering from adults, will have a very difficult time developing the confidence to become a competent, risk-taking problem solver. The pampered, dependent learner will not even consider tackling this often painful and frustrating task because of the discomfort it causes. We need to trust our children to use their own abilities to work their way through their discomfort, watching from a distance and being prepared to rescue only if absolutely necessary. We need to be very aware of our own role in our children's learning, as well as the role of the teacher to whom we delegate a large portion of the job of educating them, and we all need to work as a team.

The idea of allowing our children to tolerate discomfort and frustration can be somewhat daunting, especially if our own goals for them are to keep them happy and comfortable. Watching them as they struggle, make mistakes, fall down, get up, fall down again, takes an intestinal fortitude that few of us possess. It will only be by seeing the pride on their faces when they finally do succeed, and by telling ourselves repeatedly that it is in their own best interests to suffer temporarily, that we can hope to carry this off. We need to support each other within the "team" of parents and teachers, keeping the same goal – that of autonomous learning – firmly in mind so that no one is tempted to relieve the child's discomfort by giving in and doing it for her, or letting her get away without following through. We need to support her initially incompetent efforts in a positive way, and encourage baby steps, celebrating her successes and helping her to keep going after her failures. We need to be strong enough to allow natural consequences to take effect, so that she will learn that the harder she works, the better she does. We need to trust each other, as parents, and not sabotage the plan, either because we feel sorry for the child, or because we are angry with our partner. In other words, we need the patience of Job, the wisdom of Solomon, and the hammer of Thor, all mixed in with a little humor and a lot of tolerance.

It's a good thing that we don't have to be interviewed for this job.

Note

1. Pipher, M. (1994) *Reviving Ophelia: Saving the Selves of Adolescent Girls.* New York: Ballantine Books, p.63.

PART II

The Pampered Child Syndrome: How to Manage It and How to Avoid It

9

Management and Prevention
General Objectives

The balance of this book works on the assumption that it is beneficial to help children to become mentally and physically healthy, well-adjusted members of society. Thus, we need to look at how to prevent the extreme beliefs and behaviors that define the Pampered Child Syndrome, and how to intervene when dealing with children who already match the profile, and for whom parents and professionals alike often believe it is too late. Given that the vast majority of us have aspirations for our children to be happy, enriched, competent decision makers and problem solvers, we are clearly not going to approach either prevention or intervention by abandoning these goals. Fortunately, learned behaviors can be unlearned; once we understand the pattern, we can predict it; once we predict it, we can manage it.

It is not at all the intention to imply in any way at all that parents should seek outside help if they want to manage their own children's behavior appropriately. Quite the reverse, in fact. The message is clear that any outside intervention or assistance, if required at all, should be short-term and focused on restoring both authority and responsibility for running the family to parents as quickly as possible.

The main objectives of intervention are, therefore, as follows:

- to support a family structure that provides a healthy, safe, and nurturing environment in which children can learn the skills they need to become well-adjusted, functioning adults

- to restore the balance between children's rights and the responsibilities that accompany them in order that internalized messages be realistic and applicable outside the family

- to investigate ways to ensure that parental value systems can be clarified and translated into parenting strategies that are consistent with these values

- to encourage parents to understand their own parenting styles and ways of interacting with their children, in order to maximize the likelihood of clear communication

- to examine the roles of professionals in supporting mental well-being in children and their families, and to encourage appropriate diagnostic processes if psychiatric or psychological disorders are suspected

- to assist teachers in dealing with pampered children and their parents in ways that enhance collaboration and maintain respect

- to provide some suggestions that can be useful in approaching behavioral change, once the adult infrastructures and philosophies are in place.

Whether we are reading this as a parent or a professional, all sections are relevant if we are to understand each other's role in helping our children, although some may be more applicable than others. We can then attempt to bridge the gaps, rather than fall into them.

Warning "signs" and "symptoms"

Early identification is always the key to prevention, and so it is important to be vigilant for whatever warning signs we can recognize that cue us to take action. All syndromes consist of both signs and symptoms. "Signs" are objectively observable; for example, a rash, a fever, vomiting, high blood glucose levels, a tantrum. "Symptoms" are subjectively reported; for example, a stomach ache, nausea, dizziness, feelings of sadness or anxiety. The signs and symptoms that comprise the Pampered Child Syndrome, listed in Chapter 3, are individually present in most of us and/or our children at least some of the time, so no single behavior or characteristic is sufficient cause for alarm. Nonetheless, if we keep our eyes open for signs and our ears open for these signs and symptoms, we can evaluate each one as it occurs to determine whether or not the pattern is starting to resemble the syndrome, or whether it is simply an isolated instance or passing phase. We can then determine whether any action needs to be implemented to take back a misperceived message, to correct an undesirable behavioral pattern, or to see whether what we, as parents, are doing is consistent with what we are attempting to achieve. Such ongoing monitoring is required if we are to fulfill our mandate as parents. This is what parents do. As Barbara Coloroso has said, parenting is neither time-efficient nor cost-efficient.[1] Nor is it always convenient. However, we need to be aware of some of the same lessons we are trying to teach our children: "short-term pain for long-term gain;" "a stitch in time saves nine;" and "an ounce of prevention is worth a pound of cure."

Note

1. Coloroso, B. (1994) *Kids Are Worth It! Giving Your Child the Gift of Inner Discipline.* Toronto, ON: Somerville House.

10

Restoring Balance
Breaking the Pampering Cycle

If we are to break the pampering cycle, it is most definitely up to the adults to start the process. Few, if any, children will give up the soft life, or do things the hard way, or voluntarily move into a position of discomfort. There are a number of different fronts from which to initiate the changes that are required if the desired changes in behavior and attitude are to occur and be maintained. A top-down approach is the one suggested here, making the assumption that there needs to be fundamental change in the way the family hierarchy is structured in order for the children to resume their own developmental tasks. In addition, global value systems need to be defined, so that day-to-day decision making can be rational and consistent, and so that there is less likelihood of dissenting opinions or contradictory decisions between parents. If behavioral interventions are attempted without the necessary structural and philosophical changes, any improvements will most likely be temporary, since the infrastructure and policies will not be in place to sustain them.

Restoring the family structure
Normally, when we think about restoring balance, we think about smoothing out the playing field, evening up the portions, ensuring that both sides of the see-saw are level. In the world of parenting, "balance" takes on quite a different meaning. Families are not a level playing field, nor a democracy. They are – by nature, design, and necessity – hierarchical. They require

leaders who are self-appointed, not freely elected. Important and unpopular decisions are made neither by consensus nor by majority vote. Running a family calls for *ad hoc* unilateral decisions to be made, laws to be imposed without referenda, and for some members to be more equal than others. Virginia Satir, the late, renowned, family therapist, referred to parents as "architects,"[1] and as such they have significant responsibility for designing the basic structures upon which the various elements of the family will be based. Given that home should be a safe, nurturing place for children, it is up to parents to ensure that there is as little difference as possible in behavioral expectations between the family environment and the real world outside.

Thus, when we are investigating the means by which we can avoid, or manage, the Pampered Child Syndrome, we need to be clear that what we are aiming for is a hierarchical family structure and a top-down approach, where the parents are the project managers, and the children are quite definitely not.[2] This does not mean that the children's input, opinions, and feelings are not invited nor valued; quite the reverse. However, the bottom-line responsibility within the family lies in the hands of the parents, who need to be supported and encouraged in this endeavor, rather than having their authority eroded by well-intentioned professionals, legal experts, civil libertarians, or the media. Many parents appear to have lost the confidence to parent, and are questioning their right to decide what is OK for their children and what is not, what values to teach, what behaviors to encourage or eliminate. Most importantly for the pampered child, some parents have become apologetic for saying "no."

The "management team"

By far the most important and powerful aspect of the family is the "management team." This team may consist of two parents who live together, two single parents who live apart, parents plus step-parents, one single parent, or any combination of adults whose job it is to parent the children and run the family. Understanding the roles of the individuals who constitute this team is vital in handling any conflicts or difficulties within the family unit. It is also critical to understand that children do not form part of this team. A family is not a democracy, and both the adults and children need to be aware of this. Leaders are not elected, they are self-appointed; and important decisions are not put to the vote, because a simple majority does not rule. Parental votes are weighted votes, whether or not children think that this is fair.

Many parents worry because the managers have very different styles, perceptions, and attitudes with respect to raising children, and spend countless hours, even years, trying to persuade each other to change so that their approaches are homogeneous. Rather than waste energy in this direction, it helps to remember that child-rearing is at least an 18-year-long venture. In any other aspect of life, if we were to consider hiring only two individuals to complete such a lengthy project, we would surely choose people who had as wide a range of different skills, knowledge, perceptions, and experiences as humanly possible. Thus, the task becomes more focused on the development of a common mission statement, policy decisions, and overall blueprint, rather than on personality differences between the executives. We then need to pull together to make our differences work for the family, instead of fighting against each other.

There are not too many advantages to being a single parent. However, once it is understood that, even if outnumbered, a lone manager can never be outvoted, it becomes somewhat clearer that there is no need to make each decision by committee, and that there is never a tie vote on the management team. Single parents can define their own mission statement, use their own family values to set policy, and make determinations about daily decisions without waiting for approval. The responsibility that falls on such shoulders is, however, often overwhelming, especially if it is combined with grief and the remaining aftermath of tragic loss. It is difficult for a single parent to muster the strength and resilience needed to counterbalance the pack mentality that can develop when there is more than one child to manage. And it is simply hard work to run a family alone, even if the hierarchy is uncontested.

If there has been a separation or divorce, children are in the unfortunate position of having to answer to two different managers in two different companies, often complicated by hostile takeovers and reconstituted partnerships. Despite the inherent difficulties that may impact for many years, children are able to deal with the notion that they are working two different jobs. They can deal with a variety of working conditions and management styles, provided that their two managers do not try to interfere in each other's new company and that they recognize the difficulties faced by the children as they struggle with the frequent transitions from one to the other, and strive to cope with a double life.

Separated or divorced parents of pampered children are in great danger of exacerbating the child's problems if they enter any kind of bidding war, like Lisa's parents in Chapter 2. It is so easy to "buy" a child's affection, even in families where the members of the management team like each other. When there is animosity or hostility, or the motive is to hurt a former partner or to get revenge, the competition can become brutal. Unless both parents have truly committed to work together to ensure the best interests of the children, and there is an effective communication network between them, it is quite likely to be difficult, if not impossible, to reach consensus as to how to break the pampering cycle, and some outside consultation can often be very helpful.

In a single-parent family where a child has been abandoned by the other parent, either because of death or because the parent has left, there is the added issue of feeling sympathy. Adults then attempt to compensate for the loss by intensifying attention, supplying material goods, loosening or forsaking expectations, removing limits, and all other means at their disposal to protect children from any further, avoidable discomfort. It is important to recognize in such circumstances that, for the children, the removal of familiar expectations or "signposts" will result in increased uncertainty and heightened anxiety. So our good intentions can unwittingly be contributing to further grief and confusion. Flexibility, yes. Inconsistency and unpredictability, no. Children have already had enough of that.

The arrival of a new management partner, in the form of a *de facto* or potential step-parent, will often be the catalyst for the identification of pampered children, in that an outside observer will frequently be more attuned to parent–child patterns that have become part of the fabric of the family interactions and are taken for granted as being "normal" for all those involved in them. It is the brave new partner who tackles this issue, which may be doomed to failure as feathers are ruffled and territories invaded. However, it is often possible for newcomers to begin to effect a balance to the family environment in terms of introducing a range of new, and perhaps competing, messages that can sometimes initiate change.

Competing messages

The importance of the team approach to parenting cannot be emphasized enough when it comes to dealing with children whose sense of entitlement is overly developed and who think they are the management. If parents cannot get their act together, and one continues to sabotage the process of normalizing the world for the children, it will be a longer haul. Whether the two members of the original team like each other or not, whether they live in the same house or not, or whether they have the same parenting skills or not, is not the issue.

The child needs to have the same general messages from both. When the idea that "life is tough; suck it up!" comes from one parent, while the other is moving heaven and earth to make the hole square so that the peg can fit comfortably, the child is in a dilemma, and will most likely take the easier path. However, the notion that there *are* at least two ways to look at discomfort is better than the child internalizing either message alone.

Taking back the messages received

We began this book with looking at the messages that children often receive and internalize, regardless of our intentions when we send them. We are totally unlikely to change any of our intended messages, since they are uniformly positive and important if our children are to grow into well-adjusted adults, capable of living independently in an ever-changing world. And we will not get to anywhere we want to be if we tell our children that we want them to be unhappy, bored, or deprived of stimulation; nor if we espouse unfairness, inequality, irrationality, or unilateral imposition of power as bases for parenting. So we cannot force the pendulum to the other extreme.

Instead, we need to find a way to restore balance to the messages we give our children, and the expectations we have for their behavior. In order to accomplish this, we need to provide and reinforce messages that counterbalance the originally intended ideas (see the table on the next two pages).

"Have to" or "Choose to"

When it comes to the phrase "have to," it is very helpful for parents to understand that there is one law for adults and another, different law for children. In the world of the child, there are many things that they *have* to do; in other words, they do not have a choice. This is because they are under the care and protection of trusted adults (parents, caregivers, teachers) who make decisions for them that they are not yet experienced, skilled, or mature enough to make for themselves. The adults who "make" them do things, and consequence them if they don't, actually take on full responsibility for those decisions and the consequences that follow. Pampered children may not often be exposed to this type of situation within the family, and run into difficulties when they encounter it elsewhere. So we need to be alert for this issue when exploring family practices and parenting strategies.

The very parents who would never dream of telling children they "have to" are often the same parents who pepper descriptions of their own behavior

Original intention...	Counterbalance...
We want our children to be happy and comfortable.	We want them to know that sometimes we have to suffer short-term pain in order to experience long-term gain. So we shall reassure them that they do not need to get everything they want the moment they want it, if they, in fact, get it at all. We shall teach them that patience pays off by ensuring that, wherever possible, what we have promised they will have later, they will have later. If we do not intend to give it to them, or if there is doubt that we can follow through, we shall not promise in the first place.
We want our children to be stimulated and enriched.	"Out of boredom comes creativity" (Einstein). We want them to learn to handle downtime, as well as to be able to manage in situations that are tedious, boring, or normal. We shall, therefore, not avoid such situations, but instead let them experience them.
We want our children to make their own choices.	We want them to know that there are times when there is no choice, and that some things are not negotiable. We also want them to know that it is our responsibility to protect them from their choices when those choices are dangerous, unhealthy, or immoral, and we reserve the right to prevent them from acting on those choices. When our children make their own, fully informed choices and are aware of the potential consequences, we shall not intervene. We shall do everything we can to help them accept and deal with the consequences of those decisions.
We want our children to be included in family decisions.	We recognize that children have the right to be involved in decisions that affect them. We also recognize that some decisions that may affect them are decisions that have to be made by adults and adults alone. Thus, while we shall make every effort to ensure that children are consulted when possible, important decisions will not be put to a vote. Adult opinions are weighted more heavily because adults have more knowledge, skills, and experience, and carry the ultimate responsibility for the consequences of the decisions.

Continued on next page

Original intention...	Counterbalance...
We want our children to be given reasons for things that they are asked to do.	We are willing to share reasons where reasons exist, because this helps everyone understand the philosophies behind what we do in the family. If there is no reason, we shall try to find one. There is no obligation to provide a reason that a child believes is adequate, nor is it necessary to provide a reason with which a child concurs. "Because I said so" is a good enough reason when it comes from a trusted authority figure who has the child's best interests in mind.
We want our children to be treated equally and fairly.	We recognize different needs in our children, and whenever possible will strive to meet those needs as they arise. We also recognize that it is not fair to treat our children equally, since they are then deprived of their right to individuality. We shall attempt to treat each of our children according to his or her needs. We shall also teach them that life is not always fair, and that sometimes we just have to "suck it up."
We want our children to express their feelings and be heard.	We recognize our children's right to hold an opinion and to express it when the time is appropriate. We also recognize that our children will have a range of feelings, both positive and negative, and they have the right to these. We shall provide an environment where children can express them safely. We shall teach them, however, that, while we are willing to listen to their opinions and feelings, there are times when children should be seen and not heard, especially when other people are talking or when their views are not relevant to the situation.
We want our children to have positive self-esteem.	We value our children and we want them to value themselves. However, we recognize that personally driven accomplishments, triumph over adversity, and learning from mistakes are valuable experiences that, in fact, contribute to positive self-esteem. We also recognize that humility and self-awareness are qualities that temper overly inflated self-regard.

with the same term. They talk about "having to": drive their children here, there, and everywhere; lie down with a child for hours so he'll go to sleep; pick up after the family; get up many times in the night; yell at him before he'll listen; let her use the computer; get another telephone/television for the children; get a job to pay for the children's activities; cook something different for her; and essentially subjugate themselves to everything and anything that the children want.

It is a life-changing moment for the parent who can realize that all of these are actually *choices*; that we don't *have* to; as adults, we *choose* to. Even default is a choice. I *choose* to let it happen. As an adult, I accept the consequences of my choices, and I live with them.

Telling ourselves that we choose to pick up after our children, for example, places the locus of responsibility squarely on our own shoulders. We may choose to do so because we cannot stand the mess, or we are afraid of our children's anger, or we believe we are placed on the earth to serve. The fact is, we choose to do it. Once we can own this choice, we can then take a healthy look at *why* we are making that choice over one that might actually be more consistent with what we want our children to learn (i.e., that they are competent individuals who are capable of independent, adaptive behavior). Perhaps even more importantly, ownership of the choice reduces the sometimes overwhelming sense we have of our children's power. This indicates that we are making a good start on the notion that we, the adults, may actually be the leaders in the family, rather than bowing to pressure from the junior members.

Life is fair?

"Who said life is fair?" is something most of us heard as young children, and most of us have said to our own offspring. Many parents believe strongly in treating all of their children equally, which not surprisingly sets up the internalized message that "I should always be treated equally" and results in our children becoming very effective bean-counters. Much energy is then expended by adults and children alike to ensure that what one gets, the others also get, at least in kind. One woman in her forties remembered vividly how her mother had always made a point of spending exactly the same amount of money on birthday presents for her and her three sisters, and recounted how the eldest still calls each of her siblings on their birthdays to check that she has not been shortchanged in any way. Another family will not buy a new bed for their eldest, teenaged son, because they cannot afford new beds for their other two children. Yet another insists on all four children going to bed at exactly the same time, despite an eight-year age difference between eldest and youngest.

As Scott Peck has said, "Life is difficult. Once we accept that life is difficult, life becomes easier."[3] The same is true about equality. All of us who have more than one child know how different our children are from one another, not simply in terms of personality and temperament, but also in terms of their level of need. It is not a huge stretch from this knowledge to recognize, therefore, that to be fair, one cannot treat all of our children equally. Yet we persist in trying. If we can liberate ourselves from the notion that fairness equals equality, we are then able to provide an environment for our children that will more closely reflect the world outside the family. We can then teach them that they will not get something just because everyone else has it; that they may, in fact, not get it at all, ever. We can teach them that, indeed, there is one rule for the rich and one for the poor; that some are born more equal than others; and that not everything comes to those who wait. We have the opportunity to show them that each child is valued as the individual he or she actually is, and send messages about self-worth and integrity, rather than a compulsion to conform with the masses. Nice guys often finish last in the real world outside the family, and it is our job to prepare our nice guys for such scenarios.

Notes

1. Satir, V. (1972) *Peoplemaking.* Palo Alto, CA: Science and Behavioral Books Inc.

2. Mamen, M. (1997) *Who's in Charge? A Guide to Family Management.* Carp, ON: Creative Bound Inc.

3. Peck, M. Scott (1978) *The Road Less Traveled: A New Psychology of Love, Traditional Values and Spiritual Growth.* New York: Simon & Schuster, p.15.

11

Parent Matters

Somewhat surprisingly to those of us who are parents, there has been much debate about the importance of parents in the development of children. A few years ago, there was an article in *Newsweek* magazine, entitled "The Parent Trap: Are Parents Necessary?,"[1] featuring a review of Judith Rich Harris' *The Nurture Assumption: Why Children Turn Out the Way They Do; Parents Matter Less Than You Think and Peers Matter More.*[2] The gist of the author's argument was not founded in psychological theories or research, but rather was based on her own experience of raising two daughters, the first her biological child, and the second adopted as a two-month-old. The firstborn was the "good" child, following the book with respect to development and behavior, succeeding in school, and making a success of life. The second child developed many problem behaviors, became very defiant, ran away from home, was highly influenced by negative peers, and ended up in big trouble. The conclusion was drawn that, since both girls were raised in the same family, with all the same opportunities, but had turned out so very differently, parental influences were clearly irrelevant, and peers were clearly the most significant factor in determining eventual outcome. Fortunately, there was quite an outraged reaction to this hypothesis, both from professionals and the parenting public, since most of us who have or work with children understand that no two children actually experience the "same" family environment, that genetics are extremely important, and that parents do, indeed, matter. A recent book by Canadian psychologist Gordon Neufeld and physician Gabor Maté once again reinforces the notion that we all want to hear: that parents are, indeed, the primary and most powerful influence in our children's lives, and that we should be concentrating on our basic attachment relationships in order to provide the solid foundation they so clearly require.[3]

The assumption made here is that parents quite definitely matter. In fact, we are the most powerful instrument of change in a family. Professionals can be helpful, but only in so far as we want and allow them to be. It is important for parents to recognize that professionals are the "management consultants" – hired help, whose advice we can seek, but are not obliged to follow. We cannot dump our families in their laps and expect them to be fixed without any work on our part. We need to be willing to be introspective; to examine our own personality and other characteristics that affect our interactions with others; to discuss and collaborate with our partners; to be ready to go it alone if we are forced to do so; and to remain flexible and open to changing strategies, and even values, as our children grow and mature. When our children do not like what we do, or the values we model and teach, or the behaviors we expect from them, we may review and we may change. Or we may not. If we do so, it will be because we have considered thoroughly the options we have, and decided on a particular course of action, the consequences of which we are prepared to uphold. It will not be because our children disapprove.

Diff'rent strokes, Diff'rent folks

In the late 1960s and early 1970s, Diana Baumrind and her colleagues[4] conducted some seminal research looking at child characteristics that appeared to be related to certain parenting styles. The results have been extrapolated to produce two main dimensions of parenting: one that is concerned with parental feelings toward the child, ranging on a continuum from coldness, rejection, and distance, to warmth, acceptance, and closeness; and the other that is more action-oriented, and reflects the degree to which parents use structure and rules, ranging from highly restrictive and structured to extremely permissive and unstructured. Permissiveness may indicate a dearth of rules or expectations, or it may occur within an environment that appears to have rules but, in fact, where there is only sporadic follow-through. The combination of these two dimensions results in four distinct parenting approaches.

In turn, these four different parenting styles produce distinctly different characteristics in the children who live with them, as shown in the following.

Children of dismissive parents	Children of laissez-faire parents
No respect for authority	No respect for authority
No sense of self-respect	Lack of self-discipline
No self-discipline	Independent, outgoing
Independent, street-smart	Sense of self-worth
Rebellious, disobedient	Active, assertive
Aggressive, violent	Friendly, tolerant
Delinquent	Expectation of equality with adults
No conscience, no sense of remorse	Sense of entitlement

Children of authoritarian parents	Children of authoritative parents
Constrained by authority	Constrained by authority
Lack of self-respect, autonomy	Awareness of self
Compliant when parent present	Compliant, even when parent not present
Sullen, quarrelsome	
Inhibited	Generally well-adjusted
Inability to express feelings	Reliant on structure, dependent
Withdrawn, depressed	Polite, obedient
Lack of initiative	Sometimes submissive
	May be overprotected

It is quite readily apparent that both the dismissive and laissez-faire parenting styles are associated with a lack of recognition of or respect for authority; the former being more negatively rebellious, the latter being reminiscent of the pampered child, with the warm, loving, accepting environment nurturing an innate sense of entitlement and an expectation of equality.

Changing styles

Each of us tends to have a "preferred" parenting style, even if it is one that we aspire to, rather than practice. In reality, although we may have a particular, natural way of doing things, each individual's management style can change, not only from day to day, but also from child to child and from situation to situation. In other words, on one particular occasion with one particular child when we are in a certain mood or frame of mind, we may well be able to be authoritative. When we are being authoritative, our children are likely to exhibit the various characteristics outlined above, including polite, obedient, and well-adjusted. At another time, we may have had a bad day at work, the children may have been getting on our nerves from the moment we walk in the door – and suddenly we become authoritarian or dismissive.

As our style changes, so do the behaviors exhibited by our children. If we become authoritarian, our children become sullen, withdrawn, and hostile. If we become dismissive, they begin to act like juvenile delinquents.

Similarly, if our children are showing certain characteristics, they can influence our parenting style. When they are being independent, outgoing, and assertive, we can be laissez-faire. When they become sullen and hostile, we become authoritarian. If the shoe fits, we tend to wear it.

Add to this mix the fact that it is quite unlikely that both parents in a parenting couple have exactly the same preferred style, and the fact that our children act differently toward each of us, depending on their own intrinsic style. There is a very close, symbiotic relationship between our feelings and actions, and our children's feelings and actions. When we change, they change. When they change, we change. Our job as parents is to ensure that we keep an eye on the direction of the changes, and maintain our overall plan for running the family, rather than letting the children dictate our philosophies, and ending up with the tail wagging the dog.

Changing parenting styles for the pampered child

Using this model to help us deal with our pampered children, it is clear that withdrawal of affection and love will shift us along the "feelings" dimension from warm and accepting to cold and rejecting, and from being laissez-faire parents to being dismissive, with the resultant negative changes in our children's behavior. They may well go from being outgoing to acting out, from assertive to aggressive, and from showing initiative to being out of control. If, however, we can make the shift to being more structured and restrictive, there will be a change to the authoritative parenting approach that should result in increased compliance and better adjustment.

Many laissez-faire parents are extremely reluctant to make a shift to a more restrictive approach because they are afraid of becoming authoritarian, with the resulting sullen, withdrawn, depressive behaviors evident in their children. It is important to realize that we can indeed be more structured, and have more control over our children, without becoming authoritarian, provided we continue to supply the nurturing that they need. Structure and clear expectations within a warm, nurturing environment have consistently been shown to correlate with healthy adjustment in children of all ages.

Law and order

There are other individual personality factors that contribute to whether we are likely to be comfortable providing structure by setting expectations and rules for our children. For the half of the world born loving and needing order, the concepts of structure, routine, decisions, benchmarks, organization, and decision making are second nature. Rules help us to predict and plan our behavior and the behavior of others, and they bring a beautiful sense of tidiness to the world. Decisions reduce ambiguity and ambivalence, and enable us to tie up loose ends and get things done. Perhaps most important of all, structure reduces our anxiety, because it brings pattern to the chaos of indecision. We cannot understand why everyone would not recognize this and appreciate the opportunity to have a regulated, orderly life. We have no difficulty with the concept of including and upholding rules and expectations within our parenting style.

The remainder of the population, on the other hand, abhors order. We prefer to leave the world to unfold spontaneously, and to wait and see what happens. We are wonderful listeners, and we do not judge others. We don't want to commit to a decision, because there may be some more information forthcoming that could well change it. Thus, we prefer to maintain a very large and open "in-tray", rather than attempt to create a filing cabinet. Routines, calendars, planners, policy manuals, lists, rules – all of these leave us cold. We sense that our freedoms are threatened and our anxiety skyrockets. We sympathize and empathize with our children who seem to be stifled by the rigidity of rules, and we try hard to parent without them wherever possible. We prefer to negotiate to reach consensus, rather than to impose solutions. What if we don't have all the information…?

As with most other personality traits, we tend to be attracted to individuals who provide the balance. Those of us who are organized appreciate flexibility in others, and recognize that they somehow provide us access to the mellow side of life. Those of us who revel in our personal messes value those who bring order, make decisions, and get things done. When our differences work together, we are a wonderful team. When they clash, we call each other "anal" or "slob," and we find each other at best irritating, or at worst impossible to live with. There is no question that effective parenting requires both organization and flexibility; thus there is plenty of room for the whole continuum.

If both parents are organized decision makers, the household is quite likely to be run in a very structured way. Taken to an extreme, it may be rigid, and there may be rules for just about everything. Order may be demanded at all times, and creativity may sometimes be stifled. Parental styles are likely to be either authoritarian or authoritative. Children who crave order will instinctively be comfortable with parents who provide structure and predictability. Those children who are more flexible in nature, for whom structure produces anxiety, will need to feel safe and to trust the structure to be supportive. With two organized parents, care needs to be taken to acknowledge that inconsistency and flexibility are two different things, and that we do not have the energy to micromanage every little detail. Sometimes, this too shall pass, and the universe will unfold with or without our rules. In situations where a child's behavior requires some policing, it is relatively easy for decision makers to gear up and respond by putting rules in place and ensuring they are followed. Setting up organized structures is second nature to them, enabling them to function in their comfort zone and effectively reducing their anxiety.

But what if both parents are flexible? If they believe that rules are unnecessarily restricting? Parenting styles are likely to be much more democratic and permissive, dismissive or laissez-faire. If parents model and teach appropriate social behavior, children may well learn by observation, especially if rewarded directly or indirectly with parental approval. Expectations are less likely to be overtly stated, and rules, as such, are few and far between, or are only intermittently or arbitrarily upheld. There will be much listening and little action. Because rules are anxiety-provoking to these parents, it is much harder to get into the mindset that children need structure and order, and that these bring safety and security, as well as the predictability required to function in the world outside the family. It is thus more difficult, although not impossible, for flexible individuals to impose rules and to become more restrictive in order to bring their children's behavior under control.

The best and the worst situation is when an organized parent and a flexible parent are trying to work together as a team. Ideally, when only two people are working on a long-term, important project, it is obvious that the best combination will be individuals with skill sets that are as different from each other's as possible, so that the project will benefit from a full range of potential tools, knowledge, and experience. Then, provided they are working from the same blueprint, they can combine their expertise for the benefit of the end product. This is the best situation. The worst is when the different styles clash, and when each partner focuses on criticizing the other, and trying to change the other's style so that both match. So much energy is often invested in this goal that the product sits on the shelf, unfinished. Because of the affinity for decision making and for getting things done, the organized parent is left with all disciplinary actions and follow-through, and becomes the bad cop, while the more flexible parent is seen as the non-judging, always-listening, soft-touch. At least this combination has the advantage of watching and learning from each other. With good communication and a willingness to share the bad cop/good cop duties, the differences can be helped to work together, and a successful team can be born.

Emotional or logical decision making?

Another personality dimension that has implications for dealing with pampered children is that involving the basis for making decisions. The continuum stretches from logical analysis at one end to emotionally based decisions at the other. Parents who are more analytical will reason their way through the decision-making process in a logical fashion: if this, then that; when you have, then you may; 1–2–3; task A leads to reward B; if you push this button, here is what you will get. Although throughout the process they will most likely consider how the decision, rule, or expectation may impact on everyone, people's feelings are not the primary issue in the face of rationality. Once they have reasoned and decided, "thinking" parents will have little difficulty following through. Two "thinking" parents need to be aware of the potential effects of logic in the absence of empathy and compassion, particularly if they have managed to produce children who are more "feeling" by nature. Learning to listen to and validate children's feelings sometimes does not come easily to analytical, logical adults, since they often think that to acknowledge means to accept and to change.

Parents who tend to be more at the emotional end of this decision-making spectrum will base their choices much more on how they feel or how they believe the outcome will make others feel. If it is comfortable, they will do it. If it is not, they will not. In addition, if they feel that a particular decision will upset someone, or make someone not like them, they may choose an alternative. If a decision does upset someone, they will back off. Thus, a child who complains about being unhappy, uncomfortable, unfairly treated, hurt, upset, or disappointed is quite likely to affect the outcome of the decision-making process for a "feeling" parent. Two "feeling" parents may even be vulnerable to some emotional blackmail on the part of their children if they cannot stay connected to the logical, rational basis for parenting choices.

In parenting couples where one is logical and the other emotional, there is again the danger of the bad cop/good cop scenario. The "thinking" parent reasons his or her way through to a logical decision, and then the "feeling" parent feels sorry for the child and sabotages the plan, even if the parenting team had originally agreed. Pampered children learn very quickly who is the vulnerable parent, and will often work relentlessly to undermine the process by appealing to the emotional side.

> Jill had decided that her daughter Melanie's request for a laptop computer for her birthday was unreasonable. She already had access to a computer at both parents' houses, but was pleading for a laptop so that she could use the Internet wherever she happened to be. It was not a question of money, because they both had plenty of that, but Jill had been quite determined that Mel would not grow up thinking that money grew on trees or that she could have whatever she asked for, just because she asked for it. Mindful of the need to work as a team despite not really liking each other much, Jill had consulted Jack on the issue, presented him with all of the rational reasons she had mustered, and had persuaded him to join her in a united front, which he did, and they announced their decision together. Mel knew that it was absolutely no use asking her mother again; once Jill made up her mind and explained her reasons, it was like moving a mountain to get her to change. She just wouldn't. Mel's birthday came and went, with no laptop computer. And Mel went to work. She cuddled up to her dad; she cajoled; she pouted; she begged; she told him how mean her mom was and how she wanted to spend more time with him. Finally, she told him that if he truly loved her, he would realize how important it was for her to keep in touch with her friends. Jack simply could not bear to see her so unhappy. So he bought the laptop computer.

There is little doubt that most decisions involving our children have a large emotional component for us, and that most of us, logical or emotional, do not want to hurt our children's feelings or deliberately cause discomfort or unhappiness. However, choices based solely on whether our children like the outcome are the fodder on which pampered children feed, and it is important to develop a decision-making process that has some logical or rational basis in order to ensure that common sense prevails.

It can thus be seen that those of us who are by nature more organized and logical are perhaps less vulnerable to the whims and fancies of our children, whereas those who tend to be more flexible and feelings-based are more likely to be open to negotiation and pressure tactics. On the other side of the same coin, however, those of us who listen to and validate children's feelings may find ourselves at the warmer end of the continuum when it comes to parenting style, and are more likely to be authoritative than authoritarian, as long as we can provide the guidelines that children need in order to know what is expected of them.

There is no doubt that, regardless of our style, parents are the most powerful influences in children's lives, whether we think we are or not. This is an awesome responsibility. We know that children not only listen to the messages we send, they watch the picture, and learn from what they live. The following work,[5] written by Mary Rita Korzan, is an eloquent reminder of this reality.

When You Thought I Wasn't Looking...
By a child

When you thought I wasn't looking, I saw you hang my first painting on the refrigerator, and I immediately wanted to paint another one.

When you thought I wasn't looking, I saw you feed a stray cat, and I learned that it was good to be kind to animals.

When you thought I wasn't looking, I saw you make my favorite cake for me and I learned that the little things can be the special things in life.

When you thought I wasn't looking, I heard you say a prayer, and I knew there is a God I could always talk to and I learned to trust in God.

When you thought I wasn't looking, I saw you make a meal and take it to a friend who was sick, and I learned that we all have to help take care of each other.

When you thought I wasn't looking, I saw you give of your time and money to help people who had nothing and I learned that those who have something should give to those who don't.

When you thought I wasn't looking, I felt you kiss me good night and I felt loved and safe.

When you thought I wasn't looking, I saw you take care of our house and everyone in it and I learned we have to take care of what we are given.

When you thought I wasn't looking, I saw how you handled your responsibilities, even when you didn't feel good, and I learned that I would have to be responsible when I grow up.

When you thought I wasn't looking, I saw tears come from your eyes and learned that sometimes things hurt, but it's all right to cry.

When you thought I wasn't looking, I saw that you cared and I wanted to be everything that I could be.

When you thought I wasn't looking, I learned most of life's lessons that I need to know to be a good and productive person when I grow up.

When you thought I wasn't looking, I looked at you and wanted to say, "Thanks for all the things I saw when you thought I wasn't looking."

Each of us, parent, grandparent, relative or friend, influence the life of a child. To the world you may just be somebody, but to somebody you are the world.

From the book When You Thought I Wasn't Looking
© *Mary Rita Schilke Korzan.*
Dist. by Andrews McMeel Pulishing.
Reprinted with permission. All rights reserved.

Notes

1. Bagley, S. (1998) "The Parent Trap: Are Parents Necessary?" *Newsweek*. 3 September.

2. Harris, J. Rich (1998) *The Nurture Assumption: Why Children Turn Out the Way They Do; Parents Matter Less Than You Think and Peers Matter More*. New York: Free Press.

3. Neufeld, G. and Maté, G. (2004) *Holding on to Your Kids: Why Parents Matter*. Toronto, ON: Knopf.

4. Baumrind, D. and Black, A.E. (1967) "Socialization practices associated with dimensions of competence in preschool boys and girls." *Child Development 38*, (2), 291–327.

5. Korzan, M.R. (2004) *When You Thought I Wasn't Looking: A Lesson of Love*. Kansas, MO: Andrews McMeel Publishing.

12

Roles and Goals for Professionals

Parents are often anxious, even desperate, to explore ways to restore family harmony, or to deal with a child's unhappiness or pain, and yet may still be reluctant to seek advice or intervention from others. To admit that things are not going well at home takes both courage and humility. It is only too easy for well-meaning family members, friends, teachers, professionals, or interested others who try to give advice, to be perceived as negative and judgmental, and to alienate parents who feel forced to defend the perceived insult to their parenting abilities and to their child. It is hard not to feel blamed when everyone seems to be telling you that your child is indulged or spoiled, and essentially that you're an inept, inadequate parent, especially when you have worked so hard to find parenting strategies that are gentle, democratic, and fit with your own personality style.

It is important for all of us who may be involved in interventions of any kind, professional or personal, to approach with sensitivity any situation where we are concerned that the over-indulgence of a child is contributing to worrisome behaviors or mental health problems. The primary goals of both intervention and prevention are to support parents to continue to maintain their "management" role in the family, and to reinforce their objective of providing a safe, nurturing environment for their children. Parents know their own children better than any outsider ever will, and they are the ones who are on the front line through the ups and downs of daily life, as well as at times of family crisis, loss, trauma, and tragedy. Professionals come, and professionals go. We take maternity leave; our residency ends; we get transferred; we quit; we retire; we change professional direction; we get burned out; we get bored.

For whatever reason, we move on, sometimes after a very short time. Even if we stay the professional course, we are not on hand, in the home, when a child is trashing her room, or has woken screaming from a nightmare, or has not returned by three o'clock in the morning. Or when the adults lose their cool. Parents sometimes fly by the seats of their pants, make decisions in the heat of the emotional moment, act by their instincts, and have to live with the consequences of whatever it is they choose to do. While we can, perhaps, be of some assistance in helping parents reflect on what they would like to do, we cannot, and even arguably should not, *tell* them what to do.

Rather than attempting to present ourselves as "experts" who know better, we need to be respectful and supportive of parental goals. In this way, instead of unwittingly undermining parental credibility, we can act as "management consultants," who listen to what parents are trying to do, and who help them to do it. In this way, we can enable parents to maintain a healthy family structure, and help them to establish policies that reflect their family values, while simultaneously working to maximize their children's mental well-being. Our ultimate objective should thus be to remove ourselves from our clients' lives as soon as we possibly can, leaving the family structure solid, family values clarified, and parents confident to use their own resources to deal with whatever problems need to be resolved in order to reach their goals for their children.

Identifying the Pampered Child Syndrome

When it comes to diagnosis, there are few substitutes for standardized assessment instruments, accompanied by sound clinical experience and judgment. It is also important for those of us who are in a position to diagnose problems in children and adolescents to ensure that we check out whether parenting and/or behavioral issues are contributing to, exacerbating, or mimicking patterns of symptoms that would otherwise indicate genuine mental health disorders. There is no specific protocol available to check for the Pampered Child Syndrome. It is the answers to our regular questions, asked in the course of obtaining information regarding the presenting issue or in taking a developmental or medical history, that will clue us that it is potentially a factor to be considered. Some examples are given here that refer back to the basics of mental and physical health and well-being, as well as basic social expectations, with some of the "red flag" answers that need to be followed up with further investigation. Clearly, there are different age expectations for many of these questions or answers. The sample responses given are especially signifi-cant when the child is under 14 or 15, but even so may be important to follow up with older adolescents to see whether there is an underlying pattern or history that is related to more current concerns. Of course, there is nothing alarming about any of these responses if everything is working just fine, and neither parents nor child are experiencing difficulties. However, as profes-sionals, we are normally not involved unless there is something afoot, so we need to be alert listeners and active detectives, even if our clues lead us down dead-end alleys. (See the tables on the next five pages.)

The least we can do

It has been said that therapy has contributed in some ways to maintaining a "victim" mentality,[1] and has encouraged us to hide behind labels to avoid responsibility (as in, "I have an attention deficit disorder, so I can't help my behavior" or "Don't blame me for my credit card bill. I'm manic-depressive"). Mary Pipher[2] talks at length about the mistakes therapists make, including pathologizing normal experiences. In fact, she says:

> …all humans are fallible and all parents err. When we suggest that suf-fering can be avoided, we foster unreasonable expectations. We are sending the same message that advertisers send. Advertisers imply that suffering is unnatural, shouldn't be tolerated and can be avoided with the right products. Psychologists sometimes imply that stress-free living is possible if only we have the right tools. But in fact, all our stories have sad endings. We all die in the last act.

Fortunately, she also provides support for the positive goals of intervention with families, saying that professionals need to: be purveyors of hope and respect; teach empathy; promote authenticity and creativity; fight secrets, promote openness, and encourage facing pain directly; promote moderation and balance; foster humor; and help people build good character. We can help families to diffuse anxiety and cope with stress; control consumption, violence, and addictions; protect themselves with their values; connect to others; clarify thinking; and develop a strategy to make good decisions.

Once we have determined that there is a chance we are dealing with parental approaches and child characteristics that potentially set up the envi-ronment in which the Pampered Child Syndrome might develop, we need to look at what we can do to help parents either avoid or deal with it. It is also, of course, important that we not attribute all the signs and symptoms to

Sleeping patterns and related behaviors	"Red flag" responses
Can you tell me about your child's sleeping pattern?	• What do you mean, a pattern? • He doesn't really have a pattern; it depends.
What time does he go to bed?	• Do you mean, what time is he supposed to go to bed? • There's no set time. • Whenever he's tired. • Whenever he feels like it. • He won't go to bed until we go to bed. • It takes hours to get him to bed!
What is the bedtime routine?	• What do you mean, bedtime routine? • There is no set routine. We don't believe in imposing routine. We let him decide his own. • We all end up screaming at each other. • He argues/whines/tantrums/bargains/etc.
Does he fall asleep easily?	• He keeps coming out of his room. He won't stay in. • He insists on sleeping in our bed. • He says he's not tired.
When he is asleep, does he stay asleep all night?	• He'll often come into our room in the night. • He won't stay in his own bed. • There have been a number of times we've found him on the computer at 2 A.M. • I'll often wake up and find him in our bedroom in the morning.
What time does he wake up?	• He's supposed to get up at 7 A.M., but we have to go in several times, and then end up dragging him out of bed. • He's up at 5 A.M. every morning, downstairs watching TV, even though we tell him not to. • On the weekends, he's up early, but we can't get him up during the week!

Eating patterns and habits	"Red flag" responses
Can you tell me about your child's eating patterns?	• What do you mean, eating patterns?
How many meals a day does she eat?	• What do you mean, how many meals? • She never eats breakfast; I don't know what she eats for lunch; she'll have some supper if she likes what I'm serving; but mostly she just snacks. • I don't know.
What does she eat for breakfast?	• She doesn't eat breakfast. • I don't know. She gets her own. • A couple of cookies and a Pepsi. I tell her it's better than nothing.
What does she eat for lunch?	• I have no idea. • Nothing; her lunch always comes home untouched. • She tells me she eats what was in her lunch, but her teacher told me she has seen her throw it all in the garbage, or give it to other children. • A couple of cookies and a Pepsi. I tell her it's better than nothing.
What does she eat for supper?	• She doesn't like anything that I cook, so I have to cook something different for her. • She refuses to eat with the family, so she gets her own meals. • I don't know. She doesn't eat at home.

Continued on next page

Eating patterns and habits	"Red flag" responses
Are there any particular foods your child will not eat?	• She's a very picky eater. • I can't get her to eat any fruits or vegetables. • She's decided to become a vegetarian, so she won't eat any meat, eggs, cheese, or dairy products, just salad. • She's always on some diet or other. • She'll only eat Kraft Dinner or plain spaghetti or Kentucky Fried Chicken. • She won't try any new foods, so I have to give her the same things every day. • She'll only drink pop.
What expectations do you have about mealtimes?	• What do you mean, expectations? • None, really. We're such a busy family, we never eat together. It's every man for himself! • I know it's good for kids to have family meals together; I read that in a magazine. But no one seems to want to; they're too busy watching TV or playing on the computer. • I'd like him to eat everything on his plate, but that's such a huge battle, it's not worth it. • My husband/wife/partner doesn't get home until too late, and the kids need to eat earlier. • I try to get him to stay at the table, but he just won't. • Mealtimes just aren't a good time in our house. Somebody always ends up screaming at somebody, the kids pick at each other all the time, it's terrible. • I'm fed up with having to cook something different for everybody in the family; I just run out of ideas. • He asks what we're having and then has a fit!

Exercise, fitness and fresh air	"Red flag" responses
What does your child do as physical activity or exercise?	• What do you mean, physical activity?
	• Nothing.
	• Well, I know we all should, but we're a busy family and we just don't have the time.
	• I've tried her in everything – soccer, swimming, Tae Kwon Do, ballet, you name it. She doesn't like any of them. She goes once, then she won't go back.
	• She's a bit overweight, so exercise makes her really uncomfortable.
	• We all go biking/skating/skiing/walking, but she refuses to come.
	• She says none of her friends' parents make them do any exercise.
	• She simply will not go outside in the winter. She gets really cold. I can't make her, can I? What if she gets frostbite?
	• She doesn't like her gym teacher, so I've asked for her to be excused from gym class for the rest of the year.
What expectations do you have in the family around safety issues?	• What do you mean, safety issues?
	• It takes me ages to get him into his seatbelt.
	• He refuses to wear his bike helmet, even though I've told him he really should.
	• I'd like her to tell me whereabouts she'll be, but she says she never knows until she gets there, and then it looks dumb if she has to call home.
	• I know she's sexually active, but she totally avoids talking to me about it, so there's nothing I can do.

Continued on next page

Exercise, fitness and fresh air	"Red flag" responses
What responsibilities does your child have at home?	• What do you mean, responsibilities?
	• I've told her that I just want her to get her schoolwork done, so I don't ask her to do anything else.
	• He's so busy with his part-time job and his hockey; he simply doesn't have time for anything else.
	• She keeps saying: "I'll do it later!" but it doesn't seem to get done.
	• He says he doesn't know why he has to do chores, because I'm at home all the time and don't work.
	• I used to ask him to do things, but he doesn't do a good job, so I'd rather do it myself.
	• I get fed up with asking them over and over again. It's much easier to do it myself.

behavioral roots alone. As professionals, we have an obligation to ensure that suitable protocols have been followed to either rule in or rule out the possibility of co-existing disorders, since alternative or additional interventions may then be appropriate. Parents then frequently require even stronger encouragement to toughen up and to encourage their children to be self-sufficient, self-soothing, and self-confident, rather than self-absorbed.

As professionals, whatever our training or background, regardless of how superficially or intensively we are involved with the families we see, there are a number of goals that we can try to achieve when dealing with pampered children and their families, either in order to prevent the development of mental health disorders, or to deal with a full-blown syndrome:

1. Empathize with the difficulties parents are having.

2. Empower parents to deal with their children without the need for ongoing professional support.

3. Explore ways to build a workable family structure where adults are in charge and the children are not.

4. Examine the goals that the parents have in terms of values, messages, expectations, and behavior.

5. Educate parents with respect to normal developmental issues and age expectations.

6. Explain how expectations and goals can be adjusted within parental value systems.

7. Ensure that the strategies parents are using are consistent with their stated goals.

8. Encourage parents to explore alternative strategies that might add to their repertoire.

9. Extract ourselves from the family in an ongoing fashion.

10. Expect positive results, even if they take time to achieve.

Empathize with the difficulties parents are having

However hard we try, it is often difficult to empathize with parents who sometimes present as lacking in plain common sense when it comes to their children, despite being sensible individuals in all other areas of their lives. It is not up to us to judge whether or not whatever difficulties they are having are or are not a problem. Our perceptions are our reality, and it is our perceptions upon which we act. For a parent who is made highly anxious by an angry child, temper tantrums will be avoided at all costs, and the parent will give in rather than face a child's wrath. For a parent who is insecure, avoidance of a child's disappointment or criticism will be paramount. For a parent who was abused as a youngster, the world is not safe, and he or she will act accordingly when it comes to the children. For adults who were harshly punished or screamed at throughout childhood, there is a need to ensure that their children never experience the fear or hatred they so bitterly remember and perhaps even now harbor for their own parents.

Whether or not we agree with our clients' views of the world, it is important for all professionals to recognize that we will get nowhere unless we can establish a point of contact with parents from which we can begin to understand how life looks from within their world. Our own empathy enables us to be more effective problem solvers. But it also models for parents the possibility of not only empathizing, but also being able to balance the emotional and the rational when it comes to dealing with difficult situations.

*Empower parents to deal with their children without the need for ongoing
professional support*

Many families recruit a large number of professionals to help in acute or
chronic crisis situations. It is not that unusual to encounter a family where
there is a complete entourage of support in place: general practitioner; pediatrician; Mom's individual counselor; Dad's individual counselor; a marriage
counselor; a counselor for each of the children; and then a request for a family
counselor. Such families are centripetal, with all the energies spinning
outward and away from the core of the family. It is not uncommon in such situations for the professionals to have little, if any, contact with each other, and
therefore likely that several different philosophies will be in direct competition with each other. Even if there were a case conference held weekly, with
excellent collaboration and sharing of information, the strong message to the
parents is that they cannot function without the surrounding infrastructure,
and we end up unwittingly fragmenting and weakening the very structures we
are trying so hard to support.

We must be alert to such subtle and not-so-subtle messages regarding
people's abilities to take back their own lives. The message "You need help" is
a double-edged sword, and we must learn how to provide support from
behind the parents, rather than stepping in and taking over from them. It is,
therefore, important to discuss openly with parents that they will be supported
and assisted in the resumption of responsibility for their own family, and
encouraged to make use, if necessary, of naturally existing support networks:
each other, extended family, friends, neighbors, schools, communities, and so on.

*Explore ways to build a workable family structure where adults are in charge and
the children are not*

The mere idea that parents are the ones who are supposed to be the leaders in
the family causes shudders of horror in some people. They think immediately
of abuse of power, authoritarian methods, dictatorships, Victorian parenting,
and other images of squelching children's rights and spirits – all notions that
have been discussed earlier in this book with respect to child-centered philosophies of parenting. These beliefs need to be addressed in the context that
children are not equipped to run families, and the responsibilities given to
them for decision making and direction finding are more often than not
totally overwhelming. A four-year-old is not capable of deciding what constitutes appropriate daily nutritional intake; a ten-year-old cannot be responsible

for marital happiness; a 14-year-old is not qualified to determine whether or not the family should move in order to provide economic stability.

Children are safe when parents take the bottom-line responsibility for decisions, especially unpopular ones. They are far less anxious when they know where the signposts are on the map of their lives, and what happens when different paths are chosen. They need to know where the limits are so that they can test them occasionally to see whether they really exist or whether they are simply smoke and mirrors. Like all of us in times of chaos, they look for patterns, and are comforted and reassured when they recognize them. Most of us have worked for a boss who was insecure, incompetent, or inconsistent, and so most of us recognize how anxiety-provoking it can be when the person who is in charge of decision making abdicates that responsibility, leaves it up to us to decide, and then blames us when things go wrong. Responsibility without authority is morale-breaking. Helping parents see that children thrive when authority is exercised within a loving, nurturing environment is a very important contribution that we, as professionals, can make. Parents should not need our permission to parent, but some of them certainly need encouragement and reassurance to do so. These ideas are explored in more detail elsewhere.[3]

Examine the goals that the parents have in terms of values, messages, expectations, and behavior

If we are in a position to become a little more directly involved in parenting issues in our efforts to help break the pandering cycle, we need a model to work with, rather than relying solely on our own personal experiences. In the absence of formal family counseling or therapy training, we can at the very least take an objective, problem-solving approach. When something is not working out or going according to plan, it is natural and normal to start by asking: "What is it you are trying to achieve?" Encouraging parents to state their goals in positive terms is sometimes a challenge in the face of negative behaviors from a child. "We want him to stop..." or "We don't want her to..." are often entrenched, and assistance can often be given in rewording and reframing the goals in terms of what parents want to see more often, or what they can identify as desired behaviors. In this way, underlying values can be identified, as can issues between parents with respect to similarities and differences in overall mission statements or policy directions. In addition, it can be established whether the child yet possesses that particular desired behavior but does not exhibit it often, or whether parents have to begin by teaching it.

Most importantly, however, when parents can openly state their goals, values, and expectations, some direction is established to provide the basis for day-to-day decision making, so that parents do not always feel that they are thinking on their feet in the absence of direction from each other.

In divorced or separated families, it is still possible to do this type of work; in fact, it is my own frequent experience that all but the most extremely hostile parental "management teams" (and even some of them) have very similar overall goals for their children that can be stated clearly, when all the adult baggage can be put aside for a few moments. It is often necessary to help the parents of pampered children recognize and deal with the anxiety that this whole discussion arouses, since they are often anticipating with huge trepidation the mutiny that will undoubtedly occur once they begin to establish their authority in terms of setting the terms and conditions for the family.

Educate parents with respect to normal developmental issues and age expectations

Once goals are identified and expectations for more appropriate behavior are beginning to gel, and provided we have the appropriate education and training, it becomes possible for us to help to identify specific areas where parental expectations may well be out of line with developmental expectations, given the child's age, gender, cognitive capabilities, maturity level, emotional makeup, basic personality, and so on. At one end of the spectrum, I have encountered parents who wanted their child to "talk to a therapist about his feelings about our divorce, and to explore issues with respect to his 'inner child'" when the young boy was three years old. At the other, there are the parents who genuinely believe that a perfectly competent 16-year-old is not capable of packing her own lunch or doing her own laundry.

Given the extensive literature and politically correct sensitivities with respect to the early development of homosexuality, it is now not unusual in my practice to be asked about whether parents should worry about preschool boys who want to wear dresses, or young adolescent girls who identify more with boys as a peer group. While such parental concerns need to be taken seriously and dealt with, there is nonetheless overwhelming support for parents being the major instruments of socialization for children. It is thus very important for them to encourage behaviors that are not only socially acceptable in the environments in which their children need to function (e.g., daycare, nursery school, school, peer groups, Sunday school), but also to understand that such behaviors are well within normal expectations. It will not do a little boy any harm to be told no, that he cannot wear a dress, or a pubescent young girl to be told no, she cannot go into the boys' changing room or wear a bottom-only bathing suit – even if they want to and kick up a huge fuss when we do not let them.

There is a tremendous responsibility on professionals who are engaged in research that addresses such issues to provide a full and honest presentation of studies that purport to show results that counter popular beliefs with respect to child development, parenting issues, and family systems. It is not unusual for headlines to pick up only one small aspect of a piece of research, that alarmingly quickly becomes part of a general belief system. It certainly behoves us as professionals interacting with families on the front line to maintain our objectivity and skills in critical analysis, and to do everything we can to present a balanced view that is consistent with well-validated evidence with respect to the normal course of child development.

Explain how expectations and goals can be adjusted within parental value systems
Trying to ensure that parents are acting consistently with their own value systems is something we need to check out continuously. When we are looked to for advice, it is tempting to give it, especially if parents feel that this is what they are paying us to do. Of course, this is what relatives, friends, and others will do, solicited or unsolicited. "If I were you, I'd…" "Why don't you…" "You should…" "You shouldn't…" Sometimes, the issue and its solution are so obvious that not to give advice seems ridiculous. It is usually wise to reflect on the issue that if, in fact, it were that simple, parents would already be doing it. Therefore, if they are not, it is highly unlikely to be because they haven't thought of it before. Tackling the issue of a child who wakens crying several times in the night usually involves the advice to let the child cry it out for several nights and the issue will resolve, which, of course, it most often will. However, if one or both of the child's parents is a serious adherent of the family bed, or some attachment theory approaches to early child-rearing, such a suggestion will not only be ignored, but the baby may metaphorically be thrown out with the bath water, in that all suggestions made by the provider of such advice will be dismissed out of hand.

There is definitely an art to working with parents who have strongly entrenched value systems that may sometimes border on rigid, and this focuses on the ability to see the problem in terms of what the child's needs are in order to restore normal functioning and/or emotional stability. It is worth some effort to try to see if we can collaborate to define precisely what behaviors we desire to see, what we are trying to teach the child, and how we can best reinforce what we want. We can then often incorporate some, or if we are lucky all, of the parental values or philosophies in achieving that goal.

Many of the main objectives of good clinical training are designed to assist professionals to identify and understand our own value systems, to help us recognize when they become an issue, and to assist us in seeing when they help and when they hinder our judgment and/or clinical competence. However, there may well be situations where directly opposing value systems – our own and those of the people with whom we are working – clash so dramatically that collaborative work may simply prove impossible, even if we decide to use some professional supervision to help us deal with our own issues. It is at this point that we may need to initiate a frank, but sensitive, discussion with our clients or patients, and perhaps suggest a new referral or a different course of action. The message that "you are a hopelessly inept, crazy parent, and I simply don't know what more I can suggest because you haven't done anything I've proposed so far, even when you said you would" may not be what we intended to send, but will likely be what parents will hear. Many parents will report to subsequent therapists or counselors that previous professionals have told them that their problems are so bad that no one knows what to do. "Her teacher says he's been teaching for 35 years and has never run into a child like this." "The counselor said that it's all my fault, everything, and that I need serious help." It is important that we accept appropriate responsibility for termination of the relationship, if termination is inevitable, and that we ensure that parents are clear on what options remain available to them.

Ensure that the strategies parents are using are consistent with their stated goals

This is probably the most important intervention with respect to changing the ways in which parents are dealing with their children, particularly pampered children. When parents themselves can see that there is a real disconnect between what they actually identify as wanting for their children, and what they are currently doing to try to accomplish that goal, change becomes possible. In fact, parents will often become very motivated and impatient to establish such changes, sometimes without fully examining the more basic concepts of management team issues, mission statements, and underlying parental policy. It may be understood and agreed that, for example, they want a toddler to sleep in his own bed all night, and to feel safe doing so. They can look more objectively at the fact that they may, in fact, be exacerbating the child's fears by assuring him there must be something to be scared about, because they remove him from the situation every time he decides he needs to be. Parents can then agree to try to reduce the child's anxieties in ways other than removal from a situation they, as adults, know to be safe for him.

At older age levels, they are often still dealing with dependence/independence issues under different guises. There is the mother who wants her 20-year-old son to be more independent, to make his own decisions, and to function more maturely in second-year university, who at the same time is expecting him to e-mail her his essays before he hands them in so that she can edit them. There is also the father who complains that his 15-year-old daughter has no sense whatsoever of the value of money, who at the same time does not believe in giving her an allowance to budget, preferring instead to have her come to him asking for handouts every time she wants to buy something. Many parents complain that their children don't do what they are asked to when they are asked to, at the same time reminding, persuading, cajoling, badgering, and generally spending hours of time negotiating something that is essentially non-negotiable. We have all been there in some form or other with our own children as we parent them. Mostly, we catch ourselves, and somehow resolve the inconsistencies. It is constructive and helpful for parents to recognize that it is not helpful to beat themselves up for what they have done in the past. Once they have identified, in the here and now, that what they are doing is not working toward the goal they have now established or re-established, they have reason to try something different.

Encourage parents to explore alternative strategies that might add to their repertoire
It is all very well to help parents identify gaps in their arsenal, and may be helpful in its own right. However, most parents approach professionals in order to acquire some more weapons with which to fight the battle. In the absence of confidence in addressing this issue on our own, we can fruitfully direct parents to books, courses, conferences, workshops, support groups, other professionals, and so on. A cursory glance on the shelves at major bookstores will boggle the minds of most of us, and make it clear that there is a wealth of information out there. However, not everyone reads books, or attends parenting education events. Experience indicates that audiences for these media are overwhelmingly female, while fathers are left at home "babysitting." Using a management analogy[4] has been reasonably successful in recruiting male readers, since it uses terminology (management team, leadership, policy, procedures, conflict resolution, labor relations) that men are not sensitive about using, unlike the softer, less concrete language often used in

parenting books (empowerment, empathy, active listening, reflection). However, we have a long way to go.

Another critical issue for everyone, parents and professionals alike, to
recognize is that all children are different from each other, even those born to
the same mother and father, and even those born at the same time. A first child
is born to inexperienced, even if enthusiastic, parents, and never has the experience of an older sibling to emulate or tolerate. Some children, of course,
remain the sole child, and parents are forced to judge all their parenting experiences based on the responses of this one-off product – a situation that can
sometimes leave them wanting when it comes to reality testing, or comparing
their child to others in order to judge what is normal. A second child is, by definition, always preceded by a previous model, even if that first child tragically
has not survived, and has parents who now have some experience. This may or
may not be useful, given the propensity for second-born children to be quite
different from their older sibling, whether by accident or by design. Third-
born or subsequent children are often born to parents who are more settled,
perhaps more comfortable financially, and often more mature and less anxious
than they were with their first-born. As parents, we develop our own philosophies and methods over the years, and know what works and what doesn't
within our own families. Thus, it may be stating the obvious to note that there
are unlikely to be many parenting strategies that apply across the board to
children of all ages, with different basic temperaments and personalities, and
different genders (yes, boys and girls are different). There is clearly no single
list of parenting techniques that will apply universally, and most parents
appreciate this. They are usually quite grateful for additional suggestions,
however, that they may or may not incorporate, depending upon whether or
not they work. This said, there are some suggested strategies to be found later
on in this book that are general in nature, but provide some guidelines for
parents who wish to add to their own tool set.

Extract ourselves from the family in an ongoing fashion

Unlike most other professionals, those of us involved with mental and
physical health have as our goal our own redundancy. In other words, our job
is to do ourselves out of a job. From the very first time we meet our clients, our
objective should be to encourage their independence from us, and our intervention plan needs to incorporate the length of time we can contract to work
with the parents or family. We need to encourage them to define the problems
for us so that both we and they can understand what is going on, and then

help them to scour their own resources for tools, strategies, and ideas that already, it is hoped, exist somewhere in their repertoire that they can bring to bear to help to resolve the problems. We must avoid giving them the idea that they need to keep us around because their entrenched and complex problems will be solved only by ongoing, long-term professional support, preferably for every member of the family. This can only weaken confidence levels and exacerbate the feelings of inadequacy that so many parents already have.

The notion that psychiatrists and psychologists perpetuate themselves by expanding diagnostic categories has been discussed with some level of controversy,[5] and is about to explode again when the upcoming Fifth Edition of the *Diagnostic and Statistical Manual of the American Psychiatric Association* is published. The *DSM-V* will reportedly contain "diagnoses" that apply to relationships and families, putting more dollars in the pockets of medical professionals, and further entrenching the concept of mental illness as opposed to mental health. Worse, however, will be the strong message to parents that there must be something intrinsically wrong, that needs to be "treated" professionally, and that, sooner or later, there will be a magic pill that will somehow fix it. This is not to suggest that professionals cannot be helpful. Far from it. "Diagnosis" in its place can assist us in explaining clusters of symptoms, can give parents comfort that they are not the only ones to experience whatever they have been experiencing, and can provide us with direction for "treatment," provided treatment is what is required. Well-placed therapeutic intervention, where parents can benefit from working with a trusted, objective, experienced, well-trained, credentialed professional, can turn individuals around, can change behavior, can affect family dynamics, and improve mental health. Parents need to remain astute consumers, and professionals need to be prepared for this, and ready to justify and earn continued involvement.

Expect positive results, even if they take time to achieve

It was Henry Ford who said, "Whether you think you can, or whether you think you cannot, you are right." Even though the behaviors of the pampered child, and the parenting philosophies of their parents, often form a stable, dysfunctional dynamic that is difficult to budge, if we believe we can help, we can. Our ability to empathize, rather than to blame, and to be openly collaborative in our attempts to resolve the situation, are our best assets. If some basic shifts in philosophy or mindset can be accomplished, behavioral change can sometimes happen amazingly swiftly. Once some parents are validated for their basic belief that they would be more comfortable in charge of their own home and family, that congruence between end and means is critical, and that it is in their child's best interests to be safe within clearly stated boundaries, they can recognize unhelpful or inconsistent patterns very quickly, and competently effect the necessary adjustments. Usually, these couples, whether they are together in one home or divorced in two homes, can work together to ensure that their expectations are clearly defined, and consequences are consistently applied. They are ready to allow their children to experience the discomfort that will undoubtedly come with changing times, and empathize with it, yet support and trust their children to deal with this unhappiness, rather than backing away.

Other parenting couples need some time to adjust to the notion of trusting their children to handle negative experiences and feelings. Frequently, we need to work at the management team level for a while in order to ensure that policies are clearly in place, and *both* members of the team are on side, since sabotage is common if open discussion is not in place. Initiating work on a small behavior that does not have huge emotional impact is often the starting point, since parents of pampered children need to see that their new approach has a positive effect – otherwise they will not do it again. Baby steps. Positive reinforcement. Acknowledgement of change, however small. All of these are necessary not only for our children, but also for us, whether we are parents, professionals, or both.

Notes

1. Dineen, T. (2001) *Manufacturing Victims: What the Psychology Industry Is Doing to People.* Westmount, QC: Robert Davies Publishing.

2. Pipher, M. (1996) *The Shelter of Each Other: Rebuilding Our Families.* New York, NC: G.P. Putnam's Sons p.119.

3. Mamen, M. (1997) *Who's in Charge? A Guide to Family Management.* Carp, ON: Creative Bound Inc.

4. Mamen, M. (1997) *Who's in Charge? A Guide to Family Management.* Carp, ON: Creative Bound Inc.

5. Dineen, T. (2001) *Manufacturing Victims: What the Psychology Industry Is Doing to People.* Westmount, QC: Robert Davies Publishing.

13

A Class Act

Pampered Children and their Teachers

The front line

Caregivers and teachers are in a unique position to observe pampered children in the context of the broader environment in which these children need to function, and often we are the first to call parents' attention to the fact that their child is not adapting well to the world outside the family.

> Jesse, four, is hitting and biting other children at the daycare center whenever he doesn't get his own way, or whenever he wants something that one of the other children is already playing with.

> Tonia, six, becomes extremely distressed when she isn't first in line and when she has to wait her turn.

> Sean, five, cannot sit still for circle time.

> Neela, three, will do whatever she can to attract and maintain adult attention, to the point of destroying the daycare provider's belongings, and even attempts to hurt herself by engaging in very dangerous behaviors.

Identification of pampering is not limited to preschool experiences. There are many elementary and high school teachers who recognize the impact of years of parental indulgence, and those of us who have taught at the post-secondary level have certainly seen it, even in our third- or fourth-year classes.

Dear Mr. Robinson, Anita has not done her project because my husband was out of town, and I couldn't take her to the library last night.

Dear Ms. Robinson, thank you for your note about Joey not finishing any of his work in the classroom. I know you said he'll do it if he knows he might not be able to go out for recess unless it's done, but we believe that children have the right to play, and that recess shouldn't be held over his head just to get him to work harder. Please could you send it all home with him so that we can help him with it.

Dear Mr. Robinson, I am upset that you gave Ryan a detention for being disruptive again in your class. If you had better control over the kids, he wouldn't be allowed to behave like that.

Dear Principal Robinson, I understand that you have suspended Lisa for three days because she hit another student. You state that she had been warned several times that this would happen the next time she was involved in a physical altercation at school. She tells me that, in fact, she did not know this, and also assures me that the physical contact was accidental. I am writing to let you know that our lawyer has been contacted, and that we are considering taking action against you, the Superintendent, the Trustees, and the Ministry of Education, unless you withdraw this suspension immediately. You should know that Lisa is extremely upset by this totally unreasonable punishment and that we may well not be able to persuade her to return to school.

Dear Professor Robinson, I didn't write the mid-term three weeks ago because I was sick. I know you said we should let you know if there was any reason we couldn't write it, but I couldn't find the course outline with your phone number and e-mail address on it, and the TA wasn't in her office when I went to find her. Also the doctor at the walk-in clinic forgot to give me a letter. I need a supplemental exam. Also I need an extension on the paper because I have three other courses with projects due around the same time.

For better or for worse in such situations, parental instincts often kick in. Even though they, themselves, may be aware of and already disturbed by such behaviors at home, parents are frequently shocked and dismayed that others are judging their children and, by extension, their parenting. They leap to their own and their children's defense. Since the best defense is a good offense, they often attack the hole for being the wrong shape for their little square pegs to fit. The daycare provider is too strict; the nursery school is too regimented; the school environment stifles the child's creativity; the other children are being unreasonable; adults are being too rigid. Essentially, they strive to change the shape of the hole so that their children do not need to face the potential discomfort of having to adjust their behavior to fit the expectations of the situation. The vast majority of parents realize that adaptation to new situations is not only normal and necessary, but also healthy for children. Even the parents of pampered children are aware of this at some level; yet the discomfort that such change will produce in their children, and with which they will have to cope, is intimidating enough for them to pull out all the stops to try to fit the environment to the child, rather than struggle with the vice versa.

As teachers, we need to be aware that we can fall into the same well-intentioned trap. Even if we have confidence in our own abilities, it is easy to be ensnared in self-doubt when our teaching philosophies and/or strategies are challenged, let alone when we are personally attacked. Having parents tell us that their child is unhappy in our kindergarten class, or with how we are teaching math, or because we are being unreasonable, may well precipitate a healthy re-evaluation of what we are doing and why, potentially generating change that is based on sound judgment and is for the benefit of all our students. If we already have low confidence in our teaching abilities or in ourselves, or our competence is fragile, such a challenge from parents can precipitate a major personal life-crisis. When parents go over our heads, as they often do, and we are not supported by the school or board administration, morale tanks, and even those of us who are confident, competent teachers may give up in the face of continuing to try to swim upstream.

The result of such parental challenges may be that we back down from our considered educational philosophies in order to try to appease one particular child and his or her family. In such a circumstance, we are, in fact, reinforcing some of the same messages that the pampered child has been receiving from the world, notably that "I should never be unhappy, uncomfortable, or bored," and that "it is up to everyone else to make sure that something is done about that."

What can teachers do?

Similarly to the discussion with respect to professional roles and goals at the beginning of Chapter 12, we need to be acutely aware of two issues. First, in the words of the song, "there but for fortune go you or I," which should keep us humble, but also alert us to the fact that we may try to encourage parents to deal with their children the same way we deal with our own. The pitfalls of this are obvious to most of us who recognize that we are different parents even to each of our own children, and that what works for us in one situation will not necessarily work in another. Thus, it is unwise, let alone useless, to preach our own philosophies to other parents who have totally different upbringing, personalities, circumstances, and children. Second, parents cannot help but feel blamed when they are approached by a teacher who is perceived as being critical, whether that criticism is constructive or whether it is simply negative. We must therefore be aware of parental sensitivities and anxieties, as well as their good intentions for their children, and be willing to empathize with their concerns.

The key is *teamwork* – whether we are to make any progress in helping parents to prevent a somewhat indulged child from acquiring the full-blown Pampered Child Syndrome, or whether we are attempting to engage in damage control once a situation has reached crisis point. When all significant adults are working for the best interests of the child, it is important to identify the child's specific needs. If we can remain mature, we can accomplish this by excluding comments implying that he needs more competent parents, or that she is a spoiled brat. Instead, we can look for such general goals as:

- developing more independence in his work habits
- learning to trust authority figures to do their job
- increasing ways to interact positively with his peers
- waiting his turn
- improving his listening skills
- sharing with his peers
- contributing to the general community good, rather than his own ends
- becoming more compliant with what he is asked to do.

There is very little in this list of target behaviors to which parents will generally object, since there are most likely already similar problems to be addressed within the home situation. Establishing a connection, whereby both adult parties can feel comfortable acknowledging the opportunity to be part of the solution, is a major step to effecting some degree of change both at home and at school.

Another critical issue when it comes to teamwork is to determine the various tasks for which the different members of the team are responsible. Homework is the major focus for this issue, and is also the problem area most frequently mentioned by parents of pampered children – if not most children of school age. Homework is a contract between teacher and child, a statement of fact that is often forgotten, even by teachers. We cannot make the assumption that parents will assist a child with homework. Some will; some will not. We cannot assume that parents will allow a child to do homework him or herself. Some will; some will not. We cannot ask parents to help a child with homework – it is not a parent's job to do this. Teachers have been known to send home a note to all parents along the lines of: "We shall not have time to cover multiplication this term. Please could you ensure that your child learns the tables at home." In Ontario, relatively recent government-based educational philosophies have demanded more involvement from the parent body at large, a superficially benign philosophy that has been interpreted by some school personnel as an invitation for parents to be responsible for teaching concepts, monitoring projects, or remediating learning difficulties.

As usual, what is best for the children lies somewhere along the lines of moderation and common sense. For all children, especially those with attentional, behavioral, or learning problems, it is vital that they be encouraged to take ownership of their behavior and their school work. This is true whether the root cause is biochemical, neurological, or misperceived messages. Yes, parents need to be engaged in the process somehow, but we need to encourage the children to do their part. The table that follows shows one way in which the various subtasks of homework can be broken down, with a view to highlighting the member of the education "team" (the teacher, the parents, and the student) who is primarily responsible for each step. There are many other possibilities; individual teams can create their own system along similar lines.

Handling difficult parents

Fortunately, the vast majority of our experiences with parents will be positive, and our efforts to ensure a positive environment in which children can grow and flourish will be appreciated and reinforced. However, there are times when we are unable to satisfy parental demands to keep their children happy

Task	Teacher(s)	Student	Parents
Teaching concepts necessary for homework	**		
Setting tasks for homework	**		
Ensuring students know what is required of them	**		
Deciding how much work is reasonable	**		
Determining how much time should be spent	**		
Establishing timelines for handing in work	**		
Finding out what homework has been assigned	*	**	
Writing homework assignments in agenda	*	**	
Taking responsibility for bringing homework home		**	
Providing access to the necessary materials	**		**
Collecting the necessary materials to do the work		**	
Setting up an appropriate place to work		**	**
Making homework a priority over other activities		**	**
Ensuring there are no interruptions during homework time		**	**
Setting regular homework time		**	**
Checking in agenda to see what homework is required		**	

Task	Teacher(s)	Student	Parents
Prioritizing assignments	*	**	*
Doing the homework		**	
Checking homework for mistakes/errors		**	
Identifying specific area(s) of difficulty		**	
Exploring resources to help with area(s) of difficulty		**	
Providing assistance to clarify directions/instructions	**		*
Re-teaching concepts if necessary	**		*
Deciding whether homework is ready to hand in		**	
Handing homework in to teacher		**	
Evaluating quality of homework	**		
Providing consequences for inadequate homework	**		**

** Primary responsibility

* Can give assistance as required or requested

and entertained at all times, challenged to reach their potential, whatever that potential might be, and persuaded rather than required to carry out the various tasks inherent in a day's worth of school. There are also many important and serious issues that must be discussed, so it is essential for all parties that a forum for good communication and constructive solutions be provided.

Practical suggestions for effective parent–teacher conferences

The following guidelines are adapted from a wonderful little book called *Counseling Parents of Exceptional Children*,[1] but they also apply to parents of any child, including pampered ones. They are also discussed in more detail elsewhere as they pertain to parental approaches to parent–teacher meetings.[2]

1. Treat each individual with respect.

2. Decide in advance what needs to be accomplished. Establish the goals of identifying and planning to meet the child's needs.

3. Ask permission to take notes. It's a courtesy.

4. Begin and end with a positive and encouraging comment.

5. Don't rush the meeting. Arrange a follow-up meeting if further discussion is necessary.

6. Listen actively; reflect and acknowledge what the other party is saying.

7. Be willing to agree whenever possible.

8. Explain so that others can understand.

9. Agree on at least one action step each.

10. Summarize, plan and follow up.

It is also helpful for us to ensure that we establish a means of communicating with parents on a continuing basis, even if parents do not seem interested in doing so, and even if we are not interested in doing so. Leaving the door open and the bridge intact can go a long way to assuring a child that the adults are, indeed, willing to do their jobs, so that he can get on with his.

Don't forget the children

Having addressed the factors that are important in ensuring good communication among the adults, it is important to look at the role of the child in this scenario, especially the pampered child who believes that he or she is entitled to be treated the same as adults, that authority is something to be debated, and that life is a level playing field. It is important, therefore, to help parents to re-establish a hierarchy that takes into account such factors as seniority, responsibility, experience, knowledge, and authority. While children play a critical role in the understanding and implementation of any changes at school or home, it is important for the adult players to consult around issues of concern prior to a child being brought into the picture. It does no one's credibility any good to have parents and teachers arguing, debating each other's weaknesses or uncertainties, or even discussing each other's part in the new scheme of things, in front of the child or children involved. In fact, this weakens the adults' positions and inappropriately empowers the child. Once the adults have come to some agreement about what plans are likely to be put into place, a child's opinion can quite legitimately be sought. Adults do need to understand, of course, that seeking a child's opinion, validating that opinion, and even agreeing with that opinion, does not mandate that the child's suggestions must be implemented.

Jenny's parents have been concerned that she is not challenged in her Grade 5 classroom. Because she is verbally very precocious, her parents believe her to be intellectually "gifted" and bored in school. Her teachers have expressed discomfort at the fact that she does little or no work in class, does not seem to understand some of the concepts, and yet brings back homework that is immaculately completed and 100 percent accurate. They see her as challenging their authority in the classroom, and see her parents as overly protective, pushy and pandering.

All adult parties meet, without Jenny, although her parents are uncomfortable with this. In fact, they do not tell her that they are meeting with the teachers without her because, they say, she would be "devastated" that they would talk about her "behind her back." They manage to establish several goals for Jenny: to ensure that she completes the work she is required to do in class, even if she maintains it's "boring"; to encourage her to check with her teachers when she knows that she does not understand a concept; to have her complete as much of her homework on her own as she can, within an agreed time frame so that the teachers can more clearly monitor her understanding and her learning; and to meet again in a month's time to evaluate progress and goals. Her teachers stress the need to stick with this plan, even if Jenny doesn't agree, which everyone anticipates. In fact, they spend some time trying to think of an exhaustive list of all the potential objections that are quite likely to be raised, and all the behaviors they might expect. All the adults agree to give the plan a try for a month. Her main classroom teacher will discuss expectations with Jenny at school, and her parents will discuss the same expectations with her at home.

When her parents pluck up the courage to share this plan with Jenny, they sit down with her together to avoid the good cop/bad cop scene, and tell her that they are interested in her comments and her own suggestions. Despite this mature approach, the vast majority of their predictions come true. She rants and raves; she says how unfair everyone is; she says they can't make her; she tantrums; she sulks; she tells her parents that she hates living in this home and she's going to leave; she slams the door to her room and wails loudly. It is all that her parents can do to tolerate this level of her discomfort, and yet, somehow, the fact that they have been able to predict this per-formance has helped them to take a little step backwards and observe from the gallery.

Later, when she has calmed down, Jenny tries to explain, some-what more *logically*, that homework is useless, that she will get a much better education from reading what she wants to read and from the Internet, and that she will essentially go on strike if they try to make her work alone. Her parents listen good-naturedly, and then reflect to her what they hear. They commiserate with her dislike of homework, explaining that they do not like to do homework either. They tell her that they understand that she finds her own explorations of books and Internet sources to be more exciting and interesting; and they tell her that they, too, often feel like shutting down when someone tries to make them do something they don't want to do. They give her a few minutes to process this information, nodding quietly, and agreeing with pretty much everything she throws at them. They then explain patiently that should she decide to go on strike, a couple of things will happen: first, she will get poor marks, because they are no longer willing to do the work for her; and second, the rest of her life will go on hold until she has done what she has to do. They put much effort into holding to their part of the plan, as do Jenny's teachers.

Within the month, life has changed. As predicted, Jenny spends a few days testing the waters, and doing without access to the TV, the computer, the telephone, or her friends, to which she objects strenu-ously, but which, as her parents have indicated to her, is entirely her choice. She has had to face her teachers with work not done or unfinished, which embarrasses and upsets her. More recently, Jenny has begun to work reasonably diligently at her homework. Her parents are "on duty" for assistance, only when she can specify exactly what she needs help with and why. Her teachers have been following up by monitoring her progress closely, and providing teaching assistance where required. They have been dealing with Jenny directly if there are problems, and she has begun to respond directly to them, rather than relying on her parents to mediate for her. Her homework assignments more accurately reflect what the teachers have been observing in the classroom. She is still complaining that she is bored, and she certainly does not always like what she is asked to do. Her parents are noticing, however, that she actually seems to be quite proud of her work, even when she does not get a perfect mark, and that she is very enthusiastic about her new project, insisting that she do the research and writing up all by herself.

Well, OK, dream on! Not all stories turn out with such a happy ending. However, when the adults can stick to what they say they will do, trust is definitely established – even if slowly and reluctantly – and this sets the stage for changes in terms of the pampered child trusting herself more to tolerate the bumps and bruises encountered on the road to reality. In situations such as this, it is most often the adults, the parents or the teachers, who do not uphold our side of the bargain, perhaps because we cannot tolerate the discomfort, or are too busy, or can't be bothered, or don't receive immediate gratification for the efforts we are putting in. Familiar? Maybe. Good modeling? Definitely not. Again, we are unwittingly reinforcing some of the very messages we are trying to change. As the adults, we need to be aware of when this is occurring, and we need to practice what we preach.

The power of one

As teachers, we often feel quite helpless when we are faced with strong-minded, strong-willed, well-intentioned parents who genuinely believe they are acting in their own children's best interests, and who seem to be willing to move heaven and earth to ensure that their precious treasures are treated just as well outside the home as they are within it. Like anyone else more peripherally involved, we must recognize that it is hard enough, if not impossible, to change even those who are desperately seeking our help to change. We stand little chance of changing people who do not want to be changed. We also may find ourselves isolated, without support from colleagues, administrators, parents, and peers.

What we can do is to recognize our own individual power in the lives of the children we teach. We do not receive a lot of immediate reinforcement for what we do, and we seldom encounter former students later in life when they can look back with the 20/20 vision of hindsight and appreciate our contributions. It is, therefore, often easy to lose sight of the fact that we have tremendous potential to be a significant influence in shaping some of those important messages that will help balance the life of the pampered child.

We can structure our classrooms as benign dictatorships, where democratic principles are recognized, even if democratic rights are not always exercised, and where authority can be trusted to act fairly, even if not always equally. We can teach our students that along with rights come responsibilities, and that there is a difference between a right and a privilege. When the situation warrants, we can teach our students how to brainstorm ideas and supervise them as they work for consensus for the good of the group. We can have the confidence to set standards for behavior that take into account the developmental levels and needs of the children, while at the same time ensuring that they are acquiring the socially acceptable behaviors they will need if they are to adapt to the world in which they are trying to live. We can insist that these standards be upheld within our classroom, even when we know we have no control over what happens once the children leave. We can model those behaviors. We can treat ourselves and others with respect so that we show our students how to do that. We can ensure that there are times when children need to be seen, but not heard, and we can reinforce this positively. We can teach them the difference between feelings and behaviors, and that the two do not always match. We can let them know that there are things that have to be done, whether they want to do them or not; we can commiserate when they do not want to, but we can insist that they do. We can ensure that we provide information about their choices and the consequences of those choices, and permit them to experience them.

On the road to independence

Although this chapter has been directed at classroom teachers, it helps to remember that parents are also teachers, and therefore that everything here also applies at home. It is also important for parents and teachers alike to be aware that the goal of teaching is to transfer knowledge or skills from one person to another, so that that individual can function *independently*. Teaching is, in fact, a process, that begins with us doing something for the other person, and ends with him doing it for himself, with several intermediate steps along the way:

- *Doing* – taking responsibility for the task, with the child a passive participant or observer

- *Directing* – telling the child what to do and making sure he does it

- *Teaching* – explaining, demonstrating, modeling, and ensuring that learning is taking place

- *Helping* – prompting, questioning, supporting, and encouraging the child to take some responsibility

- *Supervising* – monitoring, observing, evaluating, refining skills if necessary
- *Delegating* – handing over responsibility to the child, while retaining responsibility for delegation
- *Letting go* – removing oneself entirely from the process.

Many of us involved with a pampered child tend to remain hooked in to the early stages of the process of teaching, and end up doing things for the child that he is perfectly competent to do for himself. We say we won't do it, but then we do. We make the excuse that it's easier, that there's less hassle, that it's quicker, that it's not worth the whining. We give up, and we give in. Most pampered children are extremely proficient at recruiting servants, whether by decree or by default, and expect to be waited on or catered to in a range of situations, including the classroom. It is quite traumatic for both the child and his servant if this relationship is terminated abruptly, since it has usually become quite an established pattern for both parties. Thus, understanding the process of letting go becomes important, so that it can be done one step at a time, rather than going from the "doing" to the "delegating" or "letting go" all at once. If we can move from "doing" to "directing," we have made progress. If we have moved too quickly, and delegated a responsibility before a child is ready to accept it, we may have to backtrack to supervising, or even right back to directing. For example, when a youngster is given the job of taking a message to the office but does not deliver it, he is clearly not yet ready for that level of responsibility. Rather than saying: "OK, then, I'll do it myself," the process approach gives the opportunity for several other intermediate options, such as teaching, monitoring, or supervising, all of which may take time, but all of which avoid the "doing" aspect that reinforces the pampered child.

It is hard on children when servants quit. And they begin to learn that good help is hard to find. They will work extremely hard to get the support back, pulling in all the resources they can find to try to avoid the anxiety that sudden independence brings. This is where we must stick to our guns, and track our position on the process of helping them become autonomous.

Notes

1. Stewart, J.C. (1978) *Counseling Parents of Exceptional Children*. Columbus, OH: Charles E. Merrill Publishing Company.
2. Mamen, M. (1998) *Laughter, Love and Limits: Parenting for Life*. Carp, ON: Creative Bound Inc., p.89.

14

Sparing the Rod without Spoiling the Child

Ten Strategies that Work

"Excellent," you may say. "This is what we've been waiting for! Now we'll find out what to do!" You may even have turned to this chapter before you would even dream of reading the rest of the book. If you are astute, and have been reading carefully, however, you will have noticed that there have been various statements made throughout about there not being any "right way" to parent, given that all children are different from each other, and that all parents have different personalities and styles. So you are perhaps surprised that any attempt is being made to suggest strategies, let alone ones that purport to "work"; and you are right to be skeptical.

The three cornerstones of research are: *understanding*, *prediction*, and *control*. Once we understand a phenomenon, we can begin to predict patterns. Once we can predict patterns, we can begin to control or manage them, even if this can only come about by changing our own behavior. These same concepts apply to parenting, teaching, and clinical practice – even to life in general. If we simply try to manage or control, without understanding, and without recognizing the patterns that help us to predict what is likely to happen, we are building our house on a shaky foundation, and our efforts are likely to collapse. So going back and reading the preceding chapters is definitely advised.

The following suggestions do not come with a money-back guarantee, and they may or may not be successful, depending upon how they are customized and implemented, and upon how consistently they are applied. They are general, rather than specific, and address approaches, rather than "rules." They are, of course, designed to control or manage children's behavior – which is a parent's job, and which becomes a teacher's job when children are placed in a classroom. There are hundreds of books containing thousands of suggestions for parents, but also there is nothing wrong with making up our own, or doing what works. It does not really matter which set of strategies we accumulate for ourselves. The main issue is our willingness to do our job, to provide safe limits for our children within which they can develop, learn, grow, and flourish, and above all, to use our common sense.

Strategy 1: Say what we mean and mean what we say

If I say I will do something and I do, or I say I will not and I don't, you can trust me. If I say I will do something but I do not, or if I say I will not but I do, you cannot trust me. If I keep saying I'm going to do something, yet I never do it, you will not only not trust me, but I will also have no credibility, and you will start to ignore everything that I say. This is very simple. It is, however, interesting that parents and teachers who do not implement this strategy wonder why the children in their care are always challenging them and trying to change their minds.

Obviously, there are occasionally going to be extenuating circumstances that cause us to change our minds, or that interfere with our ability to follow through with what we have said we will or won't do. In these circumstances, we owe the person who trusts us a reason why we are reneging on our word. As noted earlier, this reason may not be what the child wants to hear, or the child may not agree with the reason. What is at issue here is our credibility and trustworthiness.

Following through with what we have stated we will do is the means by which we set the bottom line that delineates the limit beyond which we shall not let our children go. When we ask ourselves what we would do if our child were about to run across the road in front of a speeding truck, without question the vast majority of us would reply that we would do whatever we possibly could to prevent it. We would, to a person, fling ourselves at the child, grab him, hold him even if he was resisting, restrain him, do whatever we could to physically stop the child from leaving the sidewalk. We would do this, even if the child were all grown up. We would probably do something similar to someone else's child, given the circumstances, or even an adult stranger. This gives us an immediate idea of the lengths to which we would go if someone were behaving in a way that placed him in significant peril. Would we go to this extreme if the child were to start to tease his brother or to make his way toward an object he knew he was not supposed to touch? We could, but we probably would not. Once we realize our potential capability, however, we recognize the extent of our power. The issue then becomes *where* we draw the line, not *whether* we are capable of drawing it.

Where to set this line may vary with different children in different circumstances, or it may be the same for everyone in the family, adults included. It implies that there will be tolerance up to a certain point, but beyond that point, action will be taken to ensure compliance. Parents and teachers who are nervous about following up with action may well set a bottom line that is so flexible as to be worthless. Authoritarian individuals will sometimes set a bottom line that is so rigid that there is no room at all for genuine exceptions. Good judgment is a most useful asset when determining the optimum placement of limits. Limits will differ from family to family, and perhaps even within the same family from one child to another, since developmental level, acceptance of responsibility, maturity, and need will be factors in determining specific limits that are to be set.

A child climbs on the Tomb of the Unknown Warrior, touches something he is not supposed to touch, or is misbehaving in a museum, restaurant, school bus, or other public place or event. Someone who is not the child's parent (passerby, neighbor, camp counselor, museum employee, bus driver) approaches the child, or his parents, and asks that he comply with behavioral expectations. The child's parent responds with: "But he's not doing any harm!" This may well be true. Yet, what if we set the bottom line only at the point where a child does harm? Once he has hit his little sister, destroyed something valuable, bullied another child, been expelled from school, attempted suicide, broken the law, or contributed to his parents' marital breakdown? This means that the child actually has to do harm before we will say, "Enough!" and the limit that the child internalizes is something along the lines of: "anything goes until I actually hurt someone."

We know that children need limits to show them the boundaries of acceptable behavior. All healthy children will test these limits once in a while to ascertain that they still exist, and cue us as to when they need to be re-evaluated. Those of us who work with unhappy, poorly adjusted children know that children will seek out these limits, even if it means escalating their behavior until they find them, so that they can be assured that they will not be permitted to put themselves at risk of danger or of damaging someone or something vital to their survival. Parents who set consistent limits are overall much safer for children than parents whose limits are inconsistently upheld. There is often confusion between flexibility and inconsistency. When parents maintain an overall value or expectation, but take account of extenuating circumstances, they are being flexible. An exception to the rule does not set a precedent. For example, preset bedtimes can be changed for special events, such as birthdays, school concerts or dances, or family functions. Children can cope with flexibility, since they understand that there is a basic expectation, and know that things will return to normal once the special occasion is over. Inconsistency is when parents are unclear about the underlying expectation. For example, children go to bed whenever the parents decide they need to, rather than on a set schedule. In a situation such as this, children will often argue vociferously in order to attempt to stretch the limit to a previous level, and parents may or may not give in.

Since all children will take the easiest route, and the one of least resistance, it is usually necessary to state what the bottom line is, rather than to leave it up to guesswork on the part of the child. It is also wise not to under-estimate the importance of stating the obvious. "Bedtime is nine o'clock." "Homework needs to be finished before I allow you to put the TV on." "In this family, we treat each other with respect." "I will not stand here and be spoken to in that tone of voice." "I will drive you to the party and pick you up at midnight." Since we are going to stick by what we say we will do, we need to ensure that we think before we decide what we are going to say we will do. Then we must be sure we can follow up. "I" statements are the safest in this regard, since we can certainly do what we say we are going to do.

Strategy 2: Use non-verbal behavior management strategies

How many times do we say: "I've told her again and again, but she never does anything I ask"? There is a wonderful cartoon book by Lynn Johnston entitled *If This is a Lecture, How Long Will it be?*[1] whose cover depicts her teenaged son rolling his eyes and yawning as she is flapping her lips at him. A "Far Side" cartoon shows two perspectives with respect to "What we say to dogs" and "What dogs hear," the latter of which consists of "Blah, blah, blah, Ginger." Like our pets, our children swiftly become immune to our verbalizations, but we often take a remarkably long time to recognize this. We are a verbal society, and we expect words to work to control our environment and the people in it.

Non-verbal behavior management consists of *doing* something, rather than talking about it. Our children, who believe they understand our patterns of responding, are frequently caught off-guard with such interventions, and are thus unable to muster sufficient objections or to negotiate their way out of the situation. After many weeks of asking, nagging, cajoling, badgering, threatening, and disposing of it myself, I wordlessly placed a very full, ripe compost bucket in the middle of our son's bed. His carefully considered and debated position that it had been his older sister who insisted that the family become "green," and therefore not his job to implement this policy, suddenly appeared to evaporate in the presence of the pungent aroma that now invaded his carefully guarded territory. This was more than eight years ago. He claims he can still smell it in his room. But he never needed to be reminded again.

Silently removing a child's plate at the end of a reasonable time for a meal speaks more volumes than nagging her to hurry up. Turning off a TV, unplugging a telephone, disabling a computer, removing unsuitable clothing, flushing cigarettes, serving a meal only after the dog has been fed, turning on the ignition only when the seatbelts are fastened, and other similar actions are all equally effective, and far more memorable for any child than the endless lectures that all blend into one.

If we have to speak and asking nicely does not work, single word commands ("Bed!" "Pajamas!" "Teeth!" "Supper!" "Off!") are sufficient to relay the required message without wasting precious time. If we are also using Strategy 1, we need to ensure that we follow up by ensuring that what we have said, we mean.

Non-verbal parenting accomplishes many things. We conserve energy for more enjoyable pursuits or interactions with our children; we demonstrate that actions speak louder than words; and we reinforce the notion that we are watching the picture.

Strategy 3: Clarify the difference between advice and command

If we wish to clarify communication within a family, and ensure that children know when we are serious about what we need them to do, it is important for everyone to know the difference between advice and command. A command is, by definition, something that is expected to be done, and if it is not, there is a consequence to follow. An "or else..." if you like. Essentially the child is expected to comply, with little or no choice in the matter. The command may be prefaced with "Please," as in "Please come for supper now." There are, however, times when it may sound like a request ("Would you mind...," "Would you like to...," "Do you want to...," "Please could you..."). This can be very confusing for a child, since she may answer the question with "No, thanks," or "Not right now," or "When I'm finished...," only to discover that this does not appear to be the correct response, and to find herself confronted by an irate parent. If we are to say what we mean, we need to be more direct. "Please turn the TV off now." "Please put your things away and come for supper." "It's time for homework." No less pleasing, but much more straight-forward. If we are mean what we say, we need to ensure that our commands are carried out by following through with the "...or else..." portion.

Advice, on the other hand, is given without a need to be acted upon. "It's cold outside, you might want to wear your jacket" is something we might say to our children, our spouse, or a visitor. To take our advice will bring the other person some benefit, we believe. To leave it will be the other person's loss. Advice given repeatedly is called nagging. However, if the recipient never acknowledges receipt, we may be forgiven for repeating ourselves. Advice, by definition, is not followed up with any kind of imposed consequence. We cannot say "or else you are not allowed out" if our advice to wear a jacket is not acted upon; otherwise, it has become a command.

There are many parents, especially of pampered children, who are very confused by these two concepts. Parents who deliberately choose not to impose their power are reluctant at the best of times to issue commands. Instead, they tend to make everything sound like a request or a piece of advice, and are then irritated or perplexed when their children treat what they say as if it were a request ("No, thanks," "Not right now"). Pampered children are quite used to being cajoled or persuaded, and tend to interpret even a more direct order as if it were merely a suggestion. Parents who are more definite can manage to make advice sound like an order, being particularly fond of prefacing everything with: "You should..." as in "You should talk to your boss about getting a raise," "You should get started on your project if you don't have any other homework," or "You should tell your friend you don't want to play with her if she's being mean." Children who are used to parents talking in this fashion have a difficult time with the transition to advice, since they tend to interpret everything parents say as parents telling them what to do, and they become unnecessarily hostile and defensive. It is important for both adults and children to clarify communication. "Are you asking me or telling me?"

may sound a little abrupt, but it is a legitimate question. "I'm telling you, not asking you," may also sound somewhat harsh to a pandering parent, but it shoots straight. "This is an order, not advice" or "That's advice, take it or leave it" are both legitimate statements that can help to clear up confusion. The need for clarification ensures that we, as parents or teachers, can check out our own intentions. Is it advice? Or do we mean to follow up with a consequence? If so, what is the consequence, and are we able to follow through? Do we truly mean what we say?

Strategy 4: Decide what we want to teach and teach it

Parents and teachers place much emphasis on eliminating undesirable behaviors – in other words, teaching children *not* to do something. Not only does this open up an infinite range of behaviors that we do not want children to engage in, it also involves monitoring a child until the undesirable behavior appears and then drawing attention to it. The basic rules of behavior management state that when a behavior is reinforced, it will increase in frequency. Paying attention to a behavior reinforces it. Therefore, paying attention to undesirable behaviors tends to encourage them to continue rather than to extinguish. It is critical to decide what it is we want to teach our children to do, and then to state it in positive terms. In other words, we need to tell them what we want, and not what we don't want. Once we can do this, we are in the position of having defined the behavior we want them to learn. Then we can determine the best ways to teach them this behavior. Again, this seems like a simple strategy, but is one that is frequently bypassed in our quest for more complex, persuasive techniques.

Once we have decided on what we want the child to learn, we must determine whether the child already possesses that particular skill but does not use it, or whether we need to teach him how to do it. If it is the latter, we need to study the process of learning as explained in Chapter 13, where we move from doing it for him to delegating and letting go. Once we know that the child can, in fact, produce the skill, we simply need to increase the frequency with which that skill is demonstrated.

Pampered children usually need to be taught to become appropriately independent, and to take responsibility for their choices and actions. They also do not like to be told what to do. Thus, an effective strategy that kills more than one of these birds with the same stone involves a list of accomplishments that is owned by the child. We can even incorporate the child's feelings into the list to teach them that sometimes we have to do something we would prefer not to do. It is best to choose a few simple, concrete, discrete behaviors that, once taught, will effect positive change in a number of areas. It is also important that these behaviors can be answered yes or no, rather than needing some sort of objective ranking as to how well they were performed. The list needs to be a list of "I" statements, worded in the past tense, so that the child owns them, and sees that they need to be accomplished before receiving any reinforcement.

- I got on with my homework by myself, without being reminded.
- Even though I didn't want to, I switched off the TV when I was asked.
- Even though I didn't like what was served, I ate my supper without complaining.
- I used my polite voice, even though I was angry and upset.

Once all items are checked off, the child can approach an adult – teacher or parent – for validation and simple reinforcement. "Good job," "I'm so proud of you," "You must be very proud of yourself," "Why don't you go and show Dad?" are sufficient. The rest of the child's life can then continue as planned and expected. Killing the fatted calf can wait for more monumental accomplishments than simply doing what is required.

Strategy 5: Use the "Trudeau" approach

The late Pierre Trudeau, as Canadian prime minister, invoked the War Measures Act in the fall of 1970, in response to terrorist activities by the Front de Liberation du Quebec (FLQ). This caused some consternation among journalists and others, particularly civil libertarians, and provoked one young reporter to thrust his microphone in the PM's face, asking him: "Can you tell us, Prime Minister, just how far will you go?" The unflappable Trudeau impaled the reporter with his icy blue eyes, and said in a calm voice, ringing with conviction: "Just watch me!" This needs to be our response when our children challenge us with: "You can't make me." Fortunately, like most parents, Trudeau was never tested to his limits.

Even though we know, deep down, that we cannot actually make anybody do anything they really don't want to do, we should never, ever under-estimate our own abilities, or at least our children's belief in our abilities. If we have credibility and trust, our children will believe that we are willing to follow through and "make" them, even if they have never actually seen us do it. We do not have to raise our voices; we do not have to prove ourselves. We *do* have to sound convincing, hold our heads up, make eye contact, and not blink first. When offered the choice of cleaning their rooms themselves, or having me do it, which would have involved shoveling every-thing into a plastic garbage bag that may never again have seen the light of day, my children never, ever had to think twice. All I had to do was to appear, garbage bag in hand, and offer to clean up. "No, thanks, I'll do it!" was the immediate reaction. Did I ever have to follow through? No. But, when chal-lenged with "You'd never throw our stuff out," my response of "Just watch me!" was sufficient to get them moving.

Strategy 6: Use the "Godfather" approach – make them an offer they cannot refuse

One of the best parenting strategies is to make our children an offer they cannot refuse, in that the alternatives are so horrible that they will voluntarily choose the option we would like them to pick. We will never choose "awful" if the other option is "pleasant." However, we may well choose "awful" if the other alternative is "even worse."

"Jason, you have a choice. You can either switch the TV off yourself when I tell you to, or I will switch it off. Which would you prefer?" Most children, especially those with servants, would not hesitate to have a parent do the dirty work. Hey, then he can not only feel hard done by, but can also blame and be angry with Mom or Dad. The other option may be somewhat different. "Jason, you have a choice. You can either switch the TV off yourself when I tell you to, in which case you may be allowed to switch it on the next time you ask. Or I will switch it off, in which case it will stay off for a week." This offer he may well be less likely to refuse.

There are a couple of other issues that are important when using the Godfather strategy. The first is that there are some situations in which a child has no choice, except perhaps to succumb graciously or miserably. If a child's life is full only of situations where there is no choice, he will, of course, never learn to make wise choices and good decisions. Therefore, we would expect this situation to occur only on some occasions, probably when the situation involves safety, morality, or health. Those of us who can creatively think on our feet can often come up with a choice of some kind, even if it involves a minor aspect of the situation with which we are dealing. "We are going to Grandma's." (No choice.) "Would you like to sit in the front seat or the back seat?" "Would you like to wear your red T-shirt or your blue sweater?" "Would you like to smile or frown?" The second is that we are not obliged to provide choices in situations where we require something to be done. Every parent needs to be able to say: "Because I said so!" and mean it.

In order for the parents of pampered children to use the Godfather and the Trudeau strategies appropriately and effectively, it is necessary for the mindset to be in place that parents have the right to act without their children's consent. If you have come this far in the book without getting that idea, you need to go back to the start, do not pass "Go," and do not collect the $200. If you enter a power struggle or a debate you cannot win, they will be in the position of having no one they can trust to act on their behalf and in their best interests. Please believe that your children need you to be willing to act unilaterally if necessary, so that they feel safe and secure under your protection.

Strategy 7: Use natural or logical consequences wherever possible

Natural or logical consequences are both simple and effective means of managing behavior. The beauty of natural consequences is that they are defined as whatever happens subsequent to a given action, given no artificially imposed intervention. If we leave toys out where other children are playing, they will probably be played with and perhaps misused or abused. If we are rude to someone, they may not want to spend time with us. If we insist on having our way, not sharing, or not taking turns, we will have no friends. If we run out of money, we have no means of buying anything. If we do not eat, we become more hungry. When the consequence fits the crime, an important, relevant message is sent, and we are much more likely to associate the two and remember them.

Unfortunately, some natural consequences are dangerous. If we walk in front of a moving bus, we may not survive. If we play on the street, we could be hit by a car. If we stick our finger in an electrical socket, we could be electrocuted. If we drink a 40-ounce bottle of liquor, we could get alcohol poisoning. If we have unprotected sex, we could contract a sexually transmitted disease and/or become pregnant. Parents are quite obviously and necessarily not going to permit these to happen, simply in order to teach our child a lesson. We will, therefore, impose some other consequences, should we become aware of a child's intent to engage in any of these behaviors.

Yet other natural consequences do not happen for a very long time. If we do not develop good work habits in school, we will not get good marks, and may miss out on the career opportunities we would like to have later. If we do not learn good social skills as a child, we may have difficulties in relationships later on. While parents may give lots of advice and issue warnings with respect to such long-term potential outcomes, it is not often that we wait the necessary years for them to come to fruition. Normally, we would again impose some other consequence in the meantime.

While some are simple and straightforward, finding logical consequences may require some creativity and imagination. Nonetheless, they can be very effective. If we break something that belongs to someone else, we fix it or pay to replace it. If we upset someone, we apologize. If we forget to do something, we own up and make up for it. If we are guilty, we admit fault and make restitution. The most basic logical consequence is related to what a child has to do, and what he wants to do. The life of a child falls quite nicely into the two baskets – the "have to" and the "want to." It is up to parents to determine what falls into the "have to" basket and what falls into the "want to" basket, given some input and suggestions from the children. Just because a child "wants to" does not mean that this particular activity must be included. The child can then understand very clearly that the approved, desired activities will become available to him only when he has done what he has to do. "When you have…, then you may…" is a statement of logical consequence that is simple to follow through. If a child does not complete what he has to do, he is then responsible for the lack of access to his preferred activities. Parents are in the position of being able to encourage and support, rather than punish. "Didn't you want to go out with your friends tonight? Then you'd better hurry up and finish your chores, because they're waiting for you!"

Problems arise when pampering parents try to protect children from even the most benign natural consequence, or interfere with logical ones. This means that the lesson the child learns is not the one that the natural consequences would teach, but rather that "my parents will rescue me and take over responsibility for what happens to me." Many parents truly believe that we are helping our children by protecting them. However, if our children have been encouraged to explore their options, become aware of the potential consequences of each, and make a conscious choice, interfering with that process will create uncertainty and mistrust, which is usually the opposite of what we are intending to happen.

There is, of course, an enormous variety of possible consequences to an infinite set of potential behaviors, so there is no single list that can respond to all situations. The following advice provides a simple set of expectations or principles that can provide a logical foundation for further refinement.[2]

Rules for Living
Author unknown

If you open it, close it.

If you turn it on, turn it off.

If you unlock it, lock it up.

If you break it, admit it, and fix it.

If you can't fix it, call in someone who can, and pay them at least what they are worth.

If you borrow it, return it in the same or better condition.

If you value it, take care of it.

If you make a mess, clean it up.

If you move it, put it back.

If it belongs to someone else and you want to use it, get permission.

If you don't know how to operate it, leave it alone.

If it's none of your business, don't ask questions.

If it ain't broke, don't try to fix it.

If it will tarnish someone's reputation, keep it to yourself.

If it will brighten someone's day, say it.

(Taken from *Lists to Live By* by Alice Gray)

Strategy 8: Use "I" consequences

Much to every child's surprise, there is no commandment anywhere that says parents must: lend the car; give a reason for not lending the car; spend money; give a reason for not spending our money; pick someone up on demand; drive anyone and anyone's friends anywhere; spend time or effort on anything at all, let alone for someone who cannot even be civil; or put up with any kind of abuse, even if the individual maintains that everyone else uses that kind of language. In fact, to protect our own belongings, space, time, effort, money, and dignity, we each need to have some notion of ourselves as separate, whole human beings with boundaries of our own. We have to believe that we have some self-worth and some sense of self-respect, not only for our own mental health and well-being, but also to model these for our children.

Trying to "make" someone else do something is like pushing on a string. We cannot *make* a newborn nurse on command; we cannot *make* a child sleep; we cannot *make* someone else say or do very much at all, in fact. We can ask, facilitate, reinforce, punish, ignore, demand, beg, grovel, cajole, badger, bribe, threaten, intimidate, yell, scream, hit – but we cannot *make*. The only thing we can do is to say what we mean, and do what we say. "I will not drive you," "I will pay for half," "I will not stand here and be spoken to that way," "I will count to three and then turn off the TV." "I" statements are assertive and can always be carried out.

Strategy 9: Use time outs – appropriately!

There has been much written about the use of "time out" as a means of inter-rupting negative behavior cycles. "Time out" is when a child is removed, vol-untarily or involuntarily, from a situation and given time to cool down. Time out works best when it is used as a preventative measure, rather than a punish-ment. Therefore, it is most effective when implemented very early on in an escalating cycle. Most parents read our children well. Most of us know when things are heating up. There's a certain look on the face, a particular tone of voice, increasing volume, provocative statements, and even specific situations when we know that conflict will most likely escalate – in the car, during the "witching hour" before supper, first thing in the morning. If a child can be given a second chance before the situation has gotten out of hand, the conflict may be skirted, or even avoided. This is rather like a "take two" on a movie set – complete with clapper board.

> Sean, your voice is getting loud. I'd like you to start over again with your nice voice.

> Hey, both of you! It sounds as if things are getting unpleasant. Please both go to your rooms for a little while and do something different. When you think you can play nicely, you can start over.

> Justin, please sit over there until you can be pleasant.

> OK, enough. Please leave the table, and come back when you are ready to eat properly.

> Outside! Come in again, and this time please come in quietly.

While some suggest one minute in time out per year of age, Barbara Coloroso[3] has pointed out that time out works best when, prior to being allowed out of a time out, a child is asked to come up with a strategy for behaving differently or for solving whatever problem precipitated the need for sober second thought. It is certainly important for a child of any age to spend time out in a safe space. If a time out is implemented early on, it is easier to remove a child from a conflict situation, and there is less likely to be damage done, either by a flailing child or by deliberate destructive actions. Most of us tend to wait too long before mandating a chill-out or cool-down option, and simply need to ride out the storm (ours or theirs) before trying to deal with the situation that created it.

It is important to recognize that introverted and extroverted children will use time out differently. Introverted children need time to process information, and do their best thinking when alone. They will use time out as welcome space, away from the source of conflict, to the point where they may fall asleep or forget about the conflict entirely, having come to some inner resolution or compromise. Thus, time out can provide them with a genuine opportunity for reflection and problem solving, and they will return refreshed and calmer. Telling an introverted child to "go away and come back when you have decided what to do" is, therefore, quite appropriate.

Extroverted children, on the other hand, need to process information with others, in order to share ideas, discuss options, and be validated. Interaction is thus necessary for them in order to solve problems. Time out will thus serve a totally different purpose. It will remove them from the source of their problem solving, and they will be motivated to end the time out in order to return and sort out the conflict. Telling an extroverted child to come back when the problem is solved is thus somewhat futile. Instead, they can be told to "go away and come back when you have calmed down, so we can start to talk about it and see what can be done."

Pampered children are used to having demands met instantaneously, and taking time for second thought or problem solving does not come easily. Parents who are trying to make changes need to be prepared to make some effort to get time out to work. If we give in, and do not wait for a change in behavior, or a strategy for doing things differently, or an attitude that is more acceptable, we are then reinforcing not only the original undesired behavior, but also the message that increased conflict works, and that we are ineffective as parents.

Once again, if we are to say what we mean and mean what we say, including "no," we need to ensure that our promise of a time out is kept. If we cannot, or are unwilling to, physically place a child in a time out, then we must be willing and able to time ourselves out. We can leave. We can leave physically, or we can leave emotionally. We can ignore. Many parents have voiced a concern about leaving emotionally – generally when they have had seriously emotionally distant parenting themselves, and recognize the sense of abandonment. We do need to remember that unless the child feels some discomfort, change is unlikely. But we do not want to abandon our children or cause them unnecessary pain. We need, therefore, to ensure that our children know exactly how to get us back, and that it is their choice. They can speak in a polite voice and we will listen. They can calm down and we will negotiate. They can use their words instead of their fists and we will accept them back. In other words, they can behave appropriately, and they have the power to mend what was temporarily broken.

Whether we remove a child or ourselves from a potentially conflictual situation, we need to recognize that it takes two to tango. And we need to remember that we are the adults.

Strategy 10: Act with conviction and confidence, integrity and dignity

The last thing children need is parents who are afraid of them, or who act as servants or lackeys or doormats. In these situations, the children are overwhelmed with the position of power this gives them, even though they may superficially appear to be working very hard to achieve this lofty status. In fact, they do not usually have the skills, knowledge, or experience to do the jobs they have wrestled away from the adults. More importantly, when we adults show that we are frightened of our children, or when we let them abuse us, or when we grovel or pander or simply give in to their demands, we are modeling behaviors for them that most of us are working hard to eliminate from their lives. Most parents do not want their daughters or their sons growing up accepting any kind of abuse from others, or being someone's unpaid help, or otherwise being taken advantage of or manipulated. And yet we are showing them precisely how to do this. Many of us have experienced a situation where the person we believed to be in charge and in control was, in fact, incompetent or had no backbone or was woefully inadequate in the job. When parents reveal to children that they do not know what to do, or that they have no power, or that they are scared, the natural reaction from the children is to become very stressed and alarmed, and very frightened themselves. For many children, this means an increase in their acting out or other negative behavior, primarily in order to force parents to resume the parenting role. Children will escalate their behavior until parents respond.

The reasons why a parent would let himself or herself be physically, verbally, or emotionally attacked by his or her own child are complex, and far beyond the scope of this book. Anyone reading this who finds himself or herself in such a position needs to think very carefully about exploring the situation further, not only in order to try to deal with the underlying issues of self-worth, but also, and for some perhaps more importantly, to try to understand the strong messages being delivered to the child. Such a child is at huge risk for abusing others, especially others with whom he or she develops a loving relationship. There are many women who seem to be unable to defend their own integrity and dignity, but who can be rallied to prevent their own children from perpetuating the pattern, as we know they can and probably will. If we truly want what is best for our children, we will simply not let them engage in these behaviors.

So we need to engage in some self-awareness. We can practice acting with conviction and confidence, even if we don't feel either of them inside. We can pull ourselves up to our full height, shoulders back, chin up, and walk resolutely. We can learn to turn on our heels, not just back away – or we can stand our ground in silent protest. We can get down to a child's level and look him directly in the eye. We can learn to lower our voices when we are angry, instead of raising them. We can buy time to plan what we want to say or to make decisions.

We gain confidence baby step by baby step. We need not get discouraged if at first we set the bar fairly low; at least we'll be able to surmount it. Once we've beaten the initial odds, we'll raise the bar, both for ourselves and for our children. We will see our successes only if we look for them, so we need to look for them; otherwise we will stay focused on our failures and defeats. Just as our children do, we also need reinforcement for our efforts; otherwise, we shall stop doing whatever we're doing. It is well established that we need a lot of positives in order to counteract the negatives in our lives.

We can be true to ourselves and find integrity. We can hold our heads up in front of others and find dignity. We can learn to state our own needs and wants clearly to others, including our children. We can tell others how we feel, and we can try to be part of the solution, instead of part of the problem. We can work on our other relationships – with partners, extended family, friends, co-workers, neighbors, pets, whatever. We can develop our talents and explore our passions. We can count our blessings. We can look for inspiration from within or from others. We can give of our time and energy to others. And, as we have seen so many times, we can say what we mean and mean what we say.

If we are not sure of ourselves, and need to take some time to examine our own self-esteem, the following reflection[4] can be affirming and helpful, and something to pass on to our children.

My Declaration of Self-esteem
Virginia Satir

I am me.

In all the world, there is no one else exactly like me. There are persons who have some parts like me, but no one adds up exactly like me. Therefore, everything that comes out of me is authentically mine because I alone chose it.

I own everything about me – my body, including everything it does; my mind, including all its thoughts and ideas; my eyes, including the images of all they behold; my feelings, whatever they may be – anger, joy, frustration, love, disappointment, excitement; my mouth and all the words that come out of it, polite, sweet or rough, correct or incorrect; my voice, loud or soft; and all my actions, whether they be to others or myself.

I own my fantasies, my dreams, my hopes, my fears.

I own all my triumphs and successes, all my failures and mistakes.

Because I own all of me, I can become intimately acquainted with me. By doing so, I can love me and be friendly with me in all my parts. I can make it possible for me to work in my best interests.

I know there are aspects of myself that puzzle me, and other aspects that I do not know. But as long as I am friendly and loving to myself, I can courageously and hopefully look for more solutions to the puzzles and for ways to find out more about me.

However I look and sound, whatever I say and do, and whatever I think and feel at a given moment in time is me. This is authentic and represents where I am at that moment in time.

However I looked and sounded, whatever I said and did, and however I thought and felt, some parts of me may turn out to be unfitting. I can discard that which is unfitting, and keep that which proved fitting, and invent something new for that which I discarded.

I can see, hear, feel, think, say and do. I have the tools to survive, to be close to others, to be productive, and to make sense and order out of the world of people and things outside of me.

I own me and therefore I can engineer me.

I am me and I am OK.

Notes

1. Johnston, L. (1990) *If This is a Lecture, How Long Will it be? A For Better or For Worse Collection.* Kansas, MO: Andrews McMeel Publishing.
2. Gray, A. (1999) *Lists to Live By.* Sisters, OR: Multnomah Publishers.
3. Coloroso, B. (1994) *Kids Are Worth It! Giving Your Child the Gift of Inner Discipline.* Toronto, ON: Somerville House.
4. Satir, V. (1972) *Peoplemaking.* Palo Alto, CA: Science and Behavioral Books Inc.

Happily Ever After?

Does the story of the pampered child ever have a happy ending? What happens to these children in adulthood? Is it ever too late to intervene? Sometimes yes, sometimes no; it depends; who knows? The answers are as varied as the stories themselves.

We know that we can never succeed unless we try. It is extremely hard for us as parents to watch our children suffer discomfort or pain. Yet suffer they will. They will have difficulty, need help, make mistakes, experience failure and disappointment, face tragedy and perhaps trauma, live with loss, confront challenges, meet conflict, fall down, hurt themselves, be hurt by others, have to deal with relationship breakdown, tackle illness, face death, struggle with moral dilemmas. Just the way we have or will. We recognize the impossibility of preventing any or all of these life events or passages, and some of us ask if we would, even if we could. As we mature, many of us realize that without the difficult times, it is hard to recognize and appreciate those experiences, events, relationships, that give us joy. Unlike the girl in Chapter 1, we know we need to have something to look forward to.

Success depends on so many factors. In general, the most optimistic outcomes – resulting in a reasonably well-adapted child and parents who have regained their own sense of confidence and their ability to lead and guide their family – tend to have the following aspects in common.

Adults, including parents, teachers, and significant others:

- are able to understand the factors that create the Pampered Child Syndrome

- do not waste time blaming anyone, but try to become part of the solution

- believe in the importance of family with its traditions and rituals
- recognize that neither a family nor a classroom is a democracy
- are comfortable and confident in our role as leaders
- can work together as a team
- acknowledge that socially inappropriate behavior is unacceptable, and that ignoring it condones it, and condoning it reinforces it
- believe that how we feel and what we do about that are two related but different issues
- recognize the need for empathy, altruism, and connection with a community
- teach resilience
- are willing to take back our families and accept responsibility for the "blueprint"
- recognize pandering behavior and attempt to change it
- understand that negative feelings, including grief, sadness, disappointment, anger, frustration, worry, and fear, are normal, natural, and necessary if we are to appreciate life and live it fully
- can set reasonable boundaries and limits for our children – and follow through
- say what we mean and mean what we say
- trust our children to handle discomfort
- expect our children to accept responsibility for their actions
- exercise common sense
- are able to see the difference between advice (take it or leave it) and a command (or else...)
- can determine which issues are not negotiable, and those where some choice exists
- are open and clear with our children about what we expect
- can see the humor in parenting and teaching
- recognize that being a responsible adult is not always a popularity contest

- are resilient and bend with the wind, not break
- live our values
- think seriously about what we want to teach our children and why
- understand that success is getting up one more time than we fall down
- make mistakes and learn from them
- recognize problems and seek advice when we need it
- are able to listen to advice, especially when we trust the source
- believe in ourselves and our children
- are willing and able to nurture not only others, but also ourselves
- see the difference between nurturing and indulging
- are able and willing to say: "Because I said so!" and "Who ever said life is fair?"

And remember the baby raccoons. Above all, whenever it all seems overwhelming and defeating, we, like the parents of the young girl in Chapter 1, can accept that even the longest journey begins with one small step. We then need to muster the courage to take that step, however uncomfortable it may make us, however hard we need to work, and however many mistakes we have the opportunity to learn from along the way. This is far and away the best lesson we can ever provide for our children.

Subject Index

Author Index